D0857365

Television

OPPOSING VIEWPOINTS®

Other Books of Related Interest

Television

OPPOSING VIEWPOINTS®

Jamuna Carroll, *Book Editor*

Bruce Glassman, *Vice President*
Bonnie Szumski, *Publisher*
Helen Cothran, *Managing Editor*

OPPOSING
VIEWPOINTS®
SERIES

GREENHAVEN PRESS
An imprint of Thomson Gale, a part of The Thomson Corporation

THOMSON

GALE

Detroit • New York • San Francisco • San Diego • New Haven, Conn.
Waterville, Maine • London • Munich

LIBRARY OF CONGRESS CATALOGING-IN-PUBLICATION DATA

Television / Jamuna Carroll, book editor.
    p. cm. — (Opposing viewpoints series)
Includes bibliographical references and index.
ISBN 0-7377-3338-1 (pbk. : alk. paper) — ISBN 0-7377-3337-3 (lib. : alk. paper)
    1. Television broadcasting—Social aspects—United States. I. Carroll, Jamuna.
II. Opposing viewpoints series (Unnumbered)
PN1992.6.T377 2006
302.23'45'0973—dc22
                                                                2005040152

> "Congress shall make no law...abridging the freedom of speech, or of the press."

First Amendment to the U.S. Constitution

The basic foundation of our democracy is the First Amendment guarantee of freedom of expression. The Opposing Viewpoints Series is dedicated to the concept of this basic freedom and the idea that it is more important to practice it than to enshrine it.

Contents

Why Consider
Opposing Viewpoints?

*"The only way in which a human being can make some
approach to knowing the whole of a subject is by hearing
what can be said about it by persons of every variety of
opinion and studying all modes in which it can be looked
at by every character of mind. No wise man ever
acquired his wisdom in any mode but this."*

John Stuart Mill

In our media-intensive culture it is not difficult to find differing opinions. Thousands of newspapers and magazines
and dozens of radio and television talk shows resound with
differing points of view. The difficulty lies in deciding which
opinion to agree with and which "experts" seem the most
credible. The more inundated we become with differing
opinions and claims, the more essential it is to hone critical
reading and thinking skills to evaluate these ideas. Opposing
Viewpoints books address this problem directly by presenting stimulating debates that can be used to enhance and
teach these skills. The varied opinions contained in each
book examine many different aspects of a single issue. While
examining these conveniently edited opposing views, readers
can develop critical thinking skills such as the ability to
compare and contrast authors' credibility, facts, argumenta-
tion styles, use of persuasive techniques, and other stylistic
tools. In short, the Opposing Viewpoints Series is an ideal
way to attain the higher-level thinking and reading skills so
essential in a culture of diverse and contradictory opinions.

In addition to providing a tool for critical thinking, Opposing Viewpoints books challenge readers to question their
own strongly held opinions and assumptions. Most people
form their opinions on the basis of upbringing, peer pressure, and personal, cultural, or professional bias. By reading
carefully balanced opposing views, readers must directly
confront new ideas as well as the opinions of those with
whom they disagree. This is not to simplistically argue that

everyone who reads opposing views will—or should—change his or her opinion. Instead, the series enhances readers' understanding of their own views by encouraging confrontation with opposing ideas. Careful examination of others' views can lead to the readers' understanding of the logical inconsistencies in their own opinions, perspective on why they hold an opinion, and the consideration of the possibility that their opinion requires further evaluation.

Evaluating Other Opinions

To ensure that this type of examination occurs, Opposing Viewpoints books present all types of opinions. Prominent spokespeople on different sides of each issue as well as well-known professionals from many disciplines challenge the reader. An additional goal of the series is to provide a forum for other, less known, or even unpopular viewpoints. The opinion of an ordinary person who has had to make the decision to cut off life support from a terminally ill relative, for example, may be just as valuable and provide just as much insight as a medical ethicist's professional opinion. The editors have two additional purposes in including these less known views. One, the editors encourage readers to respect others' opinions—even when not enhanced by professional credibility. It is only by reading or listening to and objectively evaluating others' ideas that one can determine whether they are worthy of consideration. Two, the inclusion of such viewpoints encourages the important critical thinking skill of objectively evaluating an author's credentials and bias. This evaluation will illuminate an author's reasons for taking a particular stance on an issue and will aid in readers' evaluation of the author's ideas.

It is our hope that these books will give readers a deeper understanding of the issues debated and an appreciation of the complexity of even seemingly simple issues when good and honest people disagree. This awareness is particularly important in a democratic society such as ours in which people enter into public debate to determine the common good. Those with whom one disagrees should not be regarded as enemies but rather as people whose views deserve careful examination and may shed light on one's own.

Thomas Jefferson once said that "difference of opinion leads to inquiry, and inquiry to truth." Jefferson, a broadly educated man, argued that "if a nation expects to be ignorant and free . . . it expects what never was and never will be." As individuals and as a nation, it is imperative that we consider the opinions of others and examine them with skill and discernment. The Opposing Viewpoints Series is intended to help readers achieve this goal.

David L. Bender and Bruno Leone,
Founders

Greenhaven Press anthologies primarily consist of previously published material taken from a variety of sources, including periodicals, books, scholarly journals, newspapers, government documents, and position papers from private and public organizations. These original sources are often edited for length and to ensure their accessibility for a young adult audience. The anthology editors also change the original titles of these works in order to clearly present the main thesis of each viewpoint and to explicitly indicate the opinion presented in the viewpoint. These alterations are made in consideration of both the reading and comprehension levels of a young adult audience. Every effort is made to ensure that Greenhaven Press accurately reflects the original intent of the authors included in this anthology.

Introduction

"Keeping an eye on your kids, banishing TV from your home, and even programming your V-chip all involve time, effort, and the possibility of conflict."
—*Jacob Sullum, senior editor of* Reason *magazine*

Sexual innuendo, profanity, and graphic violence are seemingly ubiquitous on television. Many experts claim that this content may harm young viewers, and 80 percent of American parents worry that their children are overexposed to sex and violence on TV. Not surprisingly, many parents monitor what their children watch. There are numerous opinions, however, on how adults should oversee youths' TV viewing. A few parents ban television altogether, some allow their children to watch only educational or values-driven series, and others watch and discuss questionable programming with their children. The clash over how parents should supervise their children's viewing habits is just one of many in the debate over who should regulate television and how. As many experts observe, parental monitoring, no matter the approach taken, has the advantage of avoiding the First Amendment issues that surround government censorship of televised content.

Some parents who believe that TV programming lacks value do not permit their children to watch television. They would agree with President George W. Bush's sentiment when he declared in January 2005: "They put an off button on the TV for a reason. Turn it off." According to media experts, *not* watching TV has numerous advantages—for example, it keeps youth grounded in reality. Ron Kaufman, creator of the Kill Your Television Web site, criticizes what he calls the Beautiful People Syndrome, the expectation that normal people should act and look like the unrealistically gorgeous, intelligent, wealthy, and perfect people paraded on TV. Kaufman maintains, "Beautiful People only exist on TV. Make this your mantra. . . . Rejecting the influence of TV imagery will set you on the path to enlightenment, and make *real life* so much more worthwhile." Jerry Mander, author of *Four Ar-*

guments for the Elimination of Television, explains how turning off the television restores a person's self-awareness, which he says is compromised when one watches TV:

> As you become able to pull back out of the immersion in the TV set, you can widen your perceptual environment to again include the room you are in. Your feelings and personal awareness are rekindled. With self-awareness emerging you can perceive the quality of sensory deadness television induces, the one-dimensionality of its narrowed information field, and arrive at an awareness of boredom.

Another benefit of eliminating television from the household, claim critics of TV, is that families have more time to engage in healthier, more enriching activities. One study by Thomas N. Robinson of Stanford University examined the effects of reducing the time youth spent watching television. Robinson asserts, "We had parents who said, 'This is the best thing that's happened to our family—we talk to our kids at dinnertime now.' One mother called and said her daughter used to sit at home and watch TV, and now she's found a friend down the block and they play outside every afternoon."

Other commentators, however, take issue with eliminating TV from the home entirely, pointing out that some TV programs are appropriate for youth. In order to determine which series are suitable for their children, over half of parents review audience ratings and content labels displayed at the beginning of most shows. Chosen by either the network or the show's producer, the ratings help parents decide whether youth should watch an episode by specifying the recommended minimum age of viewers as well as any offensive content that the show contains.

To ensure that children will not watch obscene programs in the absence of adults, some parents enlist the help of a V-chip, a device inside the television set that can be programmed to block certain kinds of shows. For example, the V-chip can intercept all shows that feature adult language, or any programs designed for viewers over thirteen years old. A government mandate requires that nearly all new TV sets come equipped with a V-chip, and a 2004 survey found that 15 percent of parents have used the device. Health care group the Kaiser Family Foundation describes its usefulness: "The TV ratings and the V-Chip can help parents navigate their children's way through the vast world of television. . . . The V-Chip can help parents 'screen out' the programs with TV ratings they don't want their children to watch." Former president Bill Clinton also lauds the V-chip, claiming that its development was like "handing the TV remote control back to America's parents."

Rather than censor what youth watch, some parenting experts suggest that parents watch TV shows with their children and initiate honest conversations with them about what is being shown. University of Arkansas researcher Ron Warren found that parents who are most involved in what their children watch are best able to supervise their children's viewing. Discussing with children the issues raised in TV shows is vital, Warren argues. He contends,

> Television can actually be a very useful tool for parents, especially in its ability to introduce topics that parents might find awkward or embarrassing to bring up on their own. If a TV programme depicts drug use or sex or violence, that's a golden opportunity to open a discussion with your child. That's what we call a "teachable moment."

Likewise, when it comes to TV news coverage, which many concerned parents believe is too graphic, numerous experts maintain that parents should calmly and simply explain events to their children rather than shield them from the news. In a *Reno News and Reviews* article, parent D. Brian Burghart writes, "[Am I saying] that bad news should be censored so that children will never be faced with it? No, I don't subscribe to that theory at all. I think children should have reality explained to them as soon as they are intellectually developed enough to frame the questions."

Although many parents employ the monitoring methods examined above, it is clear that none of these options prevent children from viewing violence and hearing profanity on TV at their friends' houses. While many media experts concede that parental monitoring is not perfect, they point out that it provides a reasonably effective alternative to media censorship by the government, which consistently draws fire from critics as being unconstitutional. The debate over who should protect youth from inappropriate content and how is examined along with other consequential issues in the following chapters of *Opposing Viewpoints: Television:* What Values Does Television Promote? What Are Television's Effects on Society? How Does Television Advertising Affect Society? and How Should Television Be Regulated? What role adults should play in supervising children's TV viewing will likely remain a point of controversy well into the future.

CHAPTER 1

What Values Does Television Promote?

Chapter Preface

Young reality show contestants filmed under the covers, crime scene investigators performing autopsies on bloodied bodies, teenagers portrayed as sex maniacs, and women being raped or murdered: Such scenes provoke over 90 percent of parents to conclude that television programming is too coarse. In fact, a study of prime time shows aired on basic-cable channels in 2001 found an average of twenty-two instances of sex, foul language, and violence every hour—and the average child watches 3.5 hours of television a day. Concerned that exposure to such shows may degrade children's values, religious groups and parents as well as politicians have called on broadcasting networks to produce more of what they identify as wholesome television shows such as *Joan of Arcadia* or *7th Heaven*. In these types of programs, characters are guided by morals and, when faced with tough choices, tend to make ethical decisions rather than reckless ones. Whether the majority of viewers want to watch so-called moral television, however, is hotly debated.

Broadcast producers contend that viewers are attracted to sex and violence on television and that those who want morally instructive shows can tune in to PAX and other religious networks. Indeed, programs filled with violence, gore, and sex, such as *N.Y.P.D. Blue*, *C.S.I.*, and *Desperate Housewives*, top television ratings. Leslie Moonves of Viacom, which owns CBS and UPN, notes that if people wanted to see moral and religious values portrayed on television, then "I guess we'd be seeing 'Joan of Arcadia' doing better than 'C.S.I.'" In the *New York Times*, Bill Carter proclaims that there is a great divide between what viewers say they want and what they actually want. He points to the 2004 presidential election in which voters embraced traditional cultural values and elected candidates who ran on moral platforms, including George W. Bush. In Carter's contention, these very people helped boost violent, raunchy shows to the top of the charts. He cites the Salt Lake City market, where 73 percent of the population voted for Bush. There, the top-rated TV shows at the time were *C.S.I.*, *E.R.*, and *Desperate Housewives*. Gary Schneeberger of Focus on the Family agrees that moral people often enjoy watching depravity: "History has shown that even people who could be described as values voters are prone to sinful behavior and watching representations of sinful behavior."

This view is contested, though, by analysts who believe that viewers would watch shows with moral lessons if more were available. Columnist Diana West writes that Bill Carter's assumptions about the viewing habits of people who voted based on values are flawed. For one thing, she finds fault with his evidence, stating that "values voters" are most likely not the ones who helped boost violent, smutty shows' ratings. In fact, she points out, it is possible that the 27 percent of Salt Lake City voters who did not vote for Bush were solely responsible for making those programs number one. In her opinion, people want more wholesome TV shows. Christian writer Todd Hertz is among them. Far too many television characters, he asserts, act irresponsibly and immorally by smoking, drinking, and having sex. Accordingly, he avoids watching programs that portray behavior and beliefs that run afoul of his religious principles and suggests that viewers "allow God and his Word to guide our TV and movie choices."

In response to arguments that people seeking moral television should turn to religious channels, Michael Higgins, president of St. Jerome's University, claims that "religious networks . . . are required to serve their constituency's need for informed presentation on matters mediated through their respective faiths. . . . But that does not absolve the mainstream networks from taking seriously one of the essential determinants of human meaning: religion."

The controversy over whether or not viewers really want more wholesome television programming will likely continue. Important to the debate is the question of what impact TV shows have on viewers' values. Many commentators believe that it is important to identify what values television promotes to determine whether TV shows are a positive force in people's—especially children's—lives. The authors in the following chapter theorize about the impact of television on morality.

"Two years after television was introduced to a remote city [in Canada], reports of physical aggression . . . increased 160 percent."

Televised Violence Promotes Fear and Aggression

Suzanne Chamberlin

Suzanne Chamberlin is a culture studies analyst at the Family Research Council, which promotes Christian family values. In the viewpoint that follows, she claims that television violence harms viewers, particularly children. Citing numerous studies and anecdotes, she asserts that violent TV programming encourages hostile behavior and leads people to think of the world as frightening and dangerous. Violent shows, she contends, desensitize viewers, making them more likely to believe brutality is acceptable and less likely to intervene when they witness it. Reality shows are especially deleterious, adds Chamberlin, because children think they can safely imitate aggressive, risky behavior exhibited by reality TV participants.

As you read, consider the following questions:

1. How does the author describe the "mean world" syndrome?
2. Name five types of reality TV shows, according to Chamberlin.
3. In the author's opinion, which weapons are most depicted in reality TV violence?

The majority of children's programming does not teach kids what most parents would prefer they learn. With only 14 percent of the networks' schedules devoted to children, young people often resort to adult programs that, more often than not, feature adult topics such as violence, drunkenness, and promiscuity. Even amidst shows devoted solely to children, such as cartoons, violence is the most pervasive element. According to the *Education Consumer Guide*, the incidents of violence on primetime television occur five times an hour, whereas the level of violence in Saturday morning programs is about twenty to twenty-five acts per hour. As the documentary *TV, Violence, and Youth* suggests, "Violence is a major course in TV's curriculum."

Not including the latest statistics from the "reality TV" explosion, children will be subjected to and affected by over 8,000 murders and 100,000 other acts of violence by the seventh grade, according to a study by the American Psychological Association. A *Washington Post* article suggests that evidence from over 3,000 research studies, spanning three decades, shows that the violence on television influences the attitudes and behavior of children who watch it.

Psychologist Brian Wilcox suggests that the proliferation of cruelty and brutality on television has the following effects:

Copy-Cat Violence

Some viewers will tend to directly imitate or copy aggressive behavior seen on television.

- On April 25, 2001, three young daredevils raced a car toward their friend who stood in the middle of a deserted Kentucky road. The boy, who was told to jump out of the way at the last possible second, was unable to move in time. Video cameras mounted on the car dashboard captured footage of the teenager bouncing off the hood after the automobile slammed into him. Doctors marveled that the boy survived, suffering a broken leg and internal injuries. The teenagers later admitted they were repeating a stunt they had seen on MTV's *Jackass*.
- Borrowing a phrase from the latest reality game show [*The Weakest Link*], Christopher Bishop sent a bomb to his wife in July, 2001, with the message, "You are the

weakest link, Goodbye," on the package. The bomb did explode, giving Tracy Kilgrow-Bishop minor burns.

- In October 1993, a young girl was killed in a mobile home fire that was set by her five-year-old brother, who had been watching the lead characters on *Beavis and Butthead* meddle in pyrotechnics.

- One six-year-old boy wearing a turtle costume stabbed a friend in the arm for not returning a borrowed toy. In another incident, a three-year-old boy picked up the family cat and swung it around his head like a Teenage Mutant Ninja Turtle hero wielding a weapon. When his mother tried to intervene, the boy said, "It's just like Michelangelo."

Exaggerated Fears

People who watch more violent television tend to believe that the world is a more dangerous and threatening place than those who watch less television.

- In Dr. George Gerbner's *TV Violence Profile*, Gerbner and others found that long-term regular exposure to television can contribute to people's sense of vulnerability, dependence, anxiety, and fear.

- Of the children Gerbner observed who watched six hours or more of television a day, most have grown up with the "mean world" syndrome. They feel a need to protect themselves and buy more guns, watchdogs, security systems, and locks compared to those who watch three hours of television or less per day.

Desensitization to Violence

Perhaps the most destructive and pervasive effect of television violence, desensitization causes viewers who watch repeated acts of violence to be less horrified by it in real life. Some may even develop a "bystander" mentality, in which real violence is considered unreal.

- According to author H. Featherstone in the *Harvard Education Letter*, children who watch a lot of television are less bothered by violence and less likely to see anything wrong with it. In several studies, children who watched a violent program were less quick to call for assistance or intervene when, afterwards, they saw younger children fighting.

• Leading child psychologist Dr. George Gerbner notes that children who watch violent shows are more likely to strike at a playmate, bicker, or disobey authority, and are less willing to share than those children who watch non-violent programs. A study in Canada showed that two years after television was introduced to a remote city called Notel, reports of physical aggression by children increased 160 percent.

• Researchers [Robert] Liebert and [Joyce] Sprafkin found that steady consumption of violence on television creates anti-social attitudes in all individuals and a perception that violence is the first-resort in problem solving.

• Another study by Psychologist L.R. Huesmann revisited adults who watched an above-average amount of violence on television as youths. What he found was that 59 percent of those who were interviewed as children had been involved in more than the typical number of aggressive acts later in life—

The Media Must Take Responsibility for Violent Programming

Two issues that have generated a great deal of discussion in recent years are whether the First Amendment (1) prevents government from regulating media violence to protect children or (2) prevents persons from suing the media for harms suffered because of the irresponsible manner in which violence is depicted.

I do not think the First Amendment prevents government from restricting minors' access to entertainment that glamorizes violence causing serious bodily injury or death, no matter how exploitative, gratuitous, graphic and easily imitable it is. . . .

The Supreme Court, in order to protect children, can . . . identify forms of media violence that cannot legally be shown to children, at least in the absence of a parent or guardian.

I would add that commercial portrayals of hardcore violence as entertainment and for no other reason than to make a profit, surely lie at the periphery of First Amendment concern.

I also do not think the First Amendment was intended to shield the media from all responsibility for any and all harms resulting from irresponsible portrayals of violence.

Robert Peters, panel discussion, "Sex and Violence in News and Entertainment Programming," Jersey City, NJ, April 10, 2000.

---

including domestic violence and traffic violations.

To argue that millions of people watch violent television without becoming criminals holds as much water as the argument that not all smokers get lung cancer. As Dr. Leonard Eron puts it, "The only people who dispute the connection between smoking and cancer are people in the tobacco industry. And the only people who dispute the television and violence connection are people in the entertainment industry." He goes on to say, "Television violence affects [people] of all ages, of both genders, at all socio-economic levels and all levels of intelligence. The effect is not limited to children who are already disposed to being aggressive and is not restricted to this country."

Ironically, the entertainment industry is congratulated for reducing, and in some cases eradicating, the presence of cigarettes in movies and television. In that instance, producers admitted that glamorizing them gives the wrong idea to children. But, as [author and editor] Gregg Easterbrook points out, the glamorization of firearms, which is far more dangerous, continues.

Reality TV Is Violent

Unfortunately, the rash of so-called "reality TV" has intensified the debate over television violence and promiscuity. While a wealth of research has proven dramatized violence to be harmful, few studies have measured the consequences of violent programs that represent—or purport to represent—the real world.

To discuss violence in "reality TV," it is important to first recognize the range of reality genres:

• News which excludes newscasts, but includes news magazines and news interview shows such as *Meet the Press* or *Good Morning America;*

• Tabloid news shows such as *Hard Copy;*

• Entertainment news such as *Entertainment Tonight* or *Access Hollywood;*

• Entertainment non-news shows such as *Real World, Temptation Island*, or *Unsolved Mysteries;*

• Competitive game shows such as *Survivor* or *Who Wants to Be a Millionaire;*

• Police shows such as *Cops, Top Cops,* or *Real Stories of the Highway Patrol;*
  • Documentary programs such as *Animal Kingdom* or *A & E's Biography;*
  • Talk shows such as *Jerry Springer* or *Geraldo.*

The definition of televised violence for reality programs is the same as it is for fictional programs with one exception—in reality TV, any verbal recounting of violent threats or acts are also considered in research. Previous studies have revealed that while fictional programs usually depict visual violence, reality programs tend to orally describe or report on violence instead.

Research Findings

The most prominent analyses of reality TV violence to date have been produced by the University of Texas. There the National Television Violence Study (NTVS) Research Team studied over 494 "reality" programs in the 1995–1996 season. In one year, researchers saw a 26 percent increase in the number of reality shows alone. Five years later, the amount of such programs had doubled. Their subsequent findings are as follows:

• *How much time is devoted to violence in reality programs?* Very little, according to NTVS, only two minutes of violence per show. Police programs, on the other hand, devote five times more of their broadcast to violent sequences than the average reality show. More than half of the sequences aired visual violence instead of verbal descriptions of violence.

• *What demographic is typically involved in violent sequences?* Over 70 percent of the perpetrators and victims in reality television programs were aged twenty-one to forty-four. The team also notes that a majority were of African-American descent.

• *Which weapons are typically used in reality TV's acts of violence?* Most programs show visual violence sequences involving guns, with shootings as the most common form of violence, punching and fighting ranks second. Teenagers are the most likely to use knives and commit sexual assaults. Yet for all of the police show research, NTVS recorded only one instance in fifty-three segments in which an alternative to violence was presented.

The Impact of Reality TV Is Great

Not only are there more reality shows these days and an even bigger reality show following, the violence-related content has skyrocketed. And, although relatively few research projects have focused on the American reality television phenomenon, what evidence there is suggests that realism as a feature of these shows heightens involvement, arousal, and aggression. . . .

If the audience sees an act of violence committed by an ordinary person (in place of an actor), they are more likely to feel capable of attempting something themselves. What these shows communicate to the viewer is much more deadly than the desensitization dilemma of the last three decades. Instead, the reality shows perpetuate a feeling of invincibility—which is far more dangerous than an audience that is merely less affected by violence. It breeds an "if ordinary people can do it, then I can" mentality. Meanwhile, those "ordinary people" are equipped with a number of physical and emotional safety nets unavailable and unknown to the viewers watching at home.

In other words, their televised lives are devoid of the inevitable consequences their audience would experience in duplicating what they have seen. "Real," yet sanitized.

*"Exposure to media violence alone does
not cause a child to commit a violent act,
and . . . is not the sole, or even the most
important, factor in contributing to youth
aggression."*

The Adverse Effects of Televised Violence Are Unproven

American Civil Liberties Union

The American Civil Liberties Union (ACLU) works to defend freedoms guaranteed by the Constitution. In 2004 it composed a letter, from which the following viewpoint is excerpted, to the Federal Communications Commission stating that violent TV shows do not necessarily cause viewers to become hostile. In response to charges from members of the House of Representatives that televised brutality begets violence, the ACLU counters that numerous factors, not televised violence alone, cause people to act aggressively. Violent TV programming, it points out, is protected by the First Amendment to the Constitution and often has educational value.

As you read, consider the following questions:
1. According to the Federal Trade Commission, what are the risk factors for youth violence?
2. What three examples does the ACLU give in support of its claim that violent television can have educational and social value?
3. In the ACLU's contention, what did the case *NAACP v. Claiborne Hardware Co.* conclude about First Amendment protections?

D ear Commissioner:
The ACLU [American Civil Liberties Union] submits these comments in reference to MB Docket No. 04-261, In the Matter of Violent Television Programming And Its Impact on Children. The Notice of Inquiry is long and fairly complex, seeking comment on many issues regarding violence and its effect on children, as well as the constitutionality of regulating depictions of violence. Our comments are limited to two issues: (1) the adequacy of research demonstrating the effects of violent programming; and (2) the constitutional issues in government regulation of violent programming.

The Notice of Inquiry is a response to a letter from thirty-nine members of the House of Representatives, Committee on Energy and Commerce, dated March 5, 2004. Congressional concern over media effects on children is hardly new. Each new medium is greeted with concern and efforts to regulate it on behalf of the children. The Internet is one of the most recent forms of information and entertainment causing Congressional concern, spawning several attempts to regulate the information that can reach children. Thus far, those attempts have failed, because they failed to adequately address constitutional concerns. Attempts to regulate violence in the broadcast medium are likely to meet the same fate.

Research on Television Violence Is Inconclusive

Congress often calls witnesses in hearings on media violence that opine their certainty that media violence causes violence. A dispassionate review of the data, however, demonstrates something far different.

The causes of violence are many and varied, and watching violence on television is not the sole, or even the most important factor. In September 2000, the Federal Trade Commission (FTC) issued a report entitled "Marketing Violent Entertainment to Children: A Review of the Self-Regulation and Industry Practices in the Motion Picture, Music Recording & Electronic Game Industries." In Appendix A of that report, the FTC reviewed the available research on the impact of violence in the entertainment media. Regarding causation, the FTC noted that "most researchers and investigators agree that exposure to media violence alone does not cause a

27

child to commit a violent act, and that it is not the sole, or even the most important, factor in contributing to youth aggression, anti-social attitudes, and violence."

The FTC noted that "broader research into the causes of youth violence has identified interacting risk factors, such as genetic, psychological, familial, and socioeconomic characteristics. Severe antisocial aggressive behavior appears to occur most often when more than one of these factors is present. The typical profile of a violent youth is one who comes from a troubled home, has poor cognitive skills, and exhibits psychological disorders such as anxiety, depression and attention deficit hyperactivity."

Intuitively, the conclusion that media violence causes actual violence is incorrect. While violent media is allegedly on the rise, violence, and in particular youth violence, has declined according to FBI statistics. If media violence is a causative factor, one would expect to see a rise in violent crime, rather than a decrease. . . .

Possible Benefits of Violent Television

An *amicus* brief filed on behalf of thirty-three media scholars in the case of *Interactive Digital Software Ass'n v. St. Louis County* in 2002 . . . analyzes the studies and data in the area. Quoting psychologist Guy Cumberbatch, it notes, "If one conclusion is possible, it is that the jury is not still out. It's never been in. Media violence has been subjected to lynch mob mentality with almost any evidence used to prove guilt." The brief additionally discusses the positive benefits of fantasy violence, and concludes that "censorship laws based on bogus claims that science has proved harm from violent entertainment deflect attention from the real causes of violence and, given the positive uses of violent fantasy, may be counterproductive."

Courts that have examined the data have likewise not been impressed with the proponents of causation. Most recently, a federal district court in Washington struck down a law dealing with violent video games where the violence was perpetrated against a law enforcement officer. The proponent of the law was confident that it would be upheld because it was allegedly supported by research that showed that watching violence produces violent activities. The court, however, was unimpressed, and held the law unconstitutional. [*Video Software Dealers Ass'n v. Maleng* (2004)].

Armstrong. © 1998 by United Feature Syndicate, Inc. Reproduced by permission.

Assumptions about the negative effects of viewing violence ignore the positive societal value of violent programs that teach us important lessons about history or call attention to problems that society must address. "Roots" was a national television event of enormous educational value that necessarily showed the brutality of the institution of slavery. The made-for-television movie "The Burning Bed" was credited with bringing about reform of existing spousal-abuse laws and included what some would call disturbingly violent scenes. "Saving Private Ryan" was a powerful movie about the horrors of war, and included many disturbing scenes to illustrate that point.

While those who wish to censor violence claim "hundreds of studies over decades document the harmful impact that exposure to graphic and excessive media violence has on the physical and mental health of our children," the fact remains that the basis for regulating media violence rests more on wishful thinking than hard data.

Television Violence and Strict Scrutiny

The Supreme Court has repeatedly stressed that "above all else, the First Amendment means that government has no power to restrict expression because of its message, its ideas, its subject matter, or its content." *Police Department v. Mosley* (1972). Moral and esthetic judgments are "for the individual to make, not for the Government to decree, even with the mandate or approval of the majority." *United States v. Playboy Entertainment Group, Inc.* (2000)

[According to the judges in the latter case,] the overriding justification for regulation of television violence "is the concern for the effect of the subject matter on young viewers." Clearly, any such regulation by the government would be content-based. Content-based speech restrictions are subject to strict scrutiny.

Strict scrutiny requires that any content-based speech regulation must be narrowly tailored to promote a compelling government interest. If a less restrictive alternative would serve the Government's purpose, it must use that alternative.

The fact that the studies do not generally support the thesis that media violence causes actual violence has important implications for strict scrutiny analysis. To the extent that these studies provide the "compelling government interest" in regulating television violence, they are woefully inadequate. As the FTC noted, media violence is not the sole, or even the most important factor in youth violence. Thus, there is no compelling government interest in regulating such content. . . .

Violent Television Is Protected by the Constitution

The First Amendment not only protects expression that depicts violence; it also protects speech that advocates the "use of force or violence." *NAACP v. Claiborne Hardware Co.* (1982). In *Brandenburg v. Ohio* (1969), the Supreme Court held that the government may not "forbid or proscribe advocacy of the use of force or of law violation except where such advocacy is directed to inciting or producing imminent lawless action and is likely to incite or produce such action." The Court further stated that "[a] statute which fails to draw this distinction impermissibly intrudes upon the freedoms guaranteed by the First and Fourteenth Amendments. It sweeps within its condemnation speech which our Constitution has immunized from Government control."

Applying *Brandenburg*, it is clear that television entertainment fails to meet this stringent test. Nothing in the data supports the conclusion that watching media violence will incite imminent violence. In the context of song lyrics thought to advocate minors to commit suicide, courts have found that expression enjoys full First Amendment protection. *Walker v. Osbourne* (1991). See also, *Zamora v. Columbia Broadcasting System* (1979); *DeFilippo v. National Broadcasting Co.* (1982); *Olivia N. v. National Broadcast* Co. (1981). The same result is likely for television violence.

The foregoing discussion makes it clear that (1) violent material is protected under the First Amendment; (2) because regulation of violent content is a content-based regulation, it must endure strict scrutiny; (3) there is no compelling governmental interest in regulating media violence, and therefore, any such regulation will fail under the strict scrutiny standard.

| "*What you learn from a program like* [Survivor] *is to be a skunk, to be conniving and self-seeking.*"

Reality TV Shows Encourage Immoral Behavior

Aubree Rankin

In the following viewpoint Aubree Rankin, an analyst with the Parents Television Council, contends that reality TV programs air a shocking amount of nudity, profanity, and other inappropriate behavior. According to Rankin, shows that glamorize sexual promiscuity and reward selfish, scheming contestants teach children that these qualities and behaviors are desirable. Equally worrisome, reality TV programs indicate that it is acceptable to humiliate and brutalize people as a form of entertainment, Rankin maintains. She argues that the explicit content on reality shows is even more deleterious than that on scripted series because children know it is real.

As you read, consider the following questions:
1. To what can the proliferation of reality TV shows be attributed, in the author's opinion?
2. What is Robert Peters' objection to the reward offered in reality shows such as *Survivor*?
3. What point does Rankin make about envelope-pushing television dramas?

S o-called reality programs have been around in one form or another since the earliest days of television. *Candid Camera*, considered by many to be the progenitor of today's reality series, has been around off and on since 1948. In general, reality programs are shows that capture ordinary people in unscripted, producer-contrived situations. Though the formats vary from program to program, the participants are usually taped around the clock so that cameras can record every emotional outburst, every conflict, every intimate moment, and every heart-wrenching confession for the entertainment of TV audiences. Most also involve some form of competition and the promise of cash or prizes for the winner.

Although reality series are not new to TV, it wasn't until the surprising breakout success of *Survivor* on CBS in the summer of 2000 that shows of that genre became major players in the prime time lineup. Despite critics' predictions that the fad would be short-lived, reality series have not only persisted, they have proliferated. At least 20% of the prime time schedule during the [2003] February sweeps period was composed of reality programming. From *Extreme Makeover* to *Average Joe* to *The Swan* to *The Apprentice*, it's difficult these days to turn on the television and *not* end up seeing a reality show.

The driving force behind this programming fad comes down to dollars and cents. With salaries of top TV actors topping $1 million per episode, developing new scripted series can be a risky proposition. Reality television series have low production costs and no talent to pay other than the show's host. Increasing use of product placement and prizes sponsored by corporations make some of the series virtually free to produce.

Sex, Profanity, and Selfishness Are Especially Harmful

In October 2002, the PTC [Parents Television Council] released a comprehensive study looking at this new TV phenomenon and found that reality programs in general had high levels of sexual content and foul language. Is such content any worse because it appears on a reality show than it would have been on a scripted series? There's certainly ample evidence to suggest it is.

Reality programs thrive on one-upmanship. ABC's *The*

Bachelor lets a man pick a bride out of a group of single, attractive women hand-picked by the producers. Fox's *Married by America* lets the audience pick the bride. Producers of *Big Brother* hope for a "hook-up" they can televise nationally. Fox forces couples to "hook up" or get kicked off the island on *Paradise Hotel.* Every time a reality show ups the ante with outrageous behavior or shocking footage, it's encouraging subsequent shows to add more skin, more twists, and more shocking behavior, resulting in a perpetual race to the bottom.

Gamble. © 1993 by *The Florida Times-Union.* Reproduced by permission of King Features Syndicate.

There are also legitimate concerns about the messages inherent in many of these competitions. Television serves as a model for social behavior and interaction, especially for young viewers, many of whom pick up social cues from how they see their favorite TV personalities behave. Consider the lessons those children are learning from reality programs. "What you learn from a program like [*Survivor*] is to be a skunk, to be conniving and self-seeking. These are things most parents and society generally tries to teach us we're not supposed to be. But the reward doesn't go to the best person, it goes to the biggest rat," according to Robert Peters, president of Morality in Media.

Turning Viewers into Voyeurs

Beyond content concerns, there is also widespread concern about the voyeuristic aspects of today's reality shows. Cultural criminologist Mike Presdee of the University of Sunderland says of the trend, "We're becoming a nation of voyeurs. It is cheap titillation, cheap entertainment. In *Big Brother*, people want to know if they're having sex or want to watch them going to the toilet. We know that those who brutalize others are brutalized in the process, even if it means they might well be willing to personally humiliate somebody, because they have seen it being done and think it is good fun. It is good fun, but it is also a form of mental cruelty. Domestic violence is not just physical, it includes mental violence, so what is the difference? Being cruel to somebody isn't just beating them up."

There is also growing consensus within the medical community that reality TV is bad for the contestants as well. Newcastle University (UK) psychologist Joan Harvey told the *Newcastle Journal* that she believes reality-show participants don't realize just what they're getting themselves into when they sign on to do these shows. "The contestants go into it with a certain amount of ambition but an awful lot of naivety. They are probably not as extrovert [sic] as they perceive themselves to be. They are more vulnerable than they think. When your self esteem does take a knock it can be quite catastrophic." Indeed it can. One contestant voted off the original Swedish version of *Survivor* committed suicide a short time after he returned home, prompting the producers of many reality programs to keep psychologists on staff.

Reality TV is a trend that's influencing all other areas of popular entertainment, and because such programs purport to show real people in real situations, the content can be far more explicit. Even the most envelope-pushing TV dramas wouldn't dare to use the sort of language that is constantly employed by contestants on some reality TV shows. Likewise, TV viewers watching sexual situations on scripted series know they're just watching two actors pantomiming physical intimacy. That's clearly not the case when sexual situations are presented on a reality series, making viewers voyeurs in a very real sense.

"[Survivor] provided [our family] an opportunity to talk . . . about human nature. . . . In each [contestant], we could see a reflection of our imperfect selves."

Reality TV Shows Can Have Moral Value

Greg Asimakoupoulos

Greg Asimakoupoulos is a reverend and director of creative communications for the Chapel Ministries. He suggests in the following viewpoint that reality TV programs offer parents an opportunity to discuss with their children the Bible's teachings about morality and humanity. While his family watched *Survivor* together, he asserts, they examined the contestants' beliefs, motives, and behavior. Besides gaining an understanding of human nature, he maintains, his family bonded while watching the show. He credits such rituals for strengthening marriages and families.

As you read, consider the following questions:
1. What topics does the author say he remains informed of in order to stay in touch with popular culture?
2. According to the author, how did his family prepare for the *Survivor* finale?
3. What purposes do family rituals and traditions serve, in the author's contention?

Greg Asimakoupoulos, "Why We Watched *Survivor*," *Christian Parenting Today*, vol. 13, March 2001, p. 46. Copyright © 2001 by Christianity Today, Inc. Reproduced by permission of the author.

In the jungle of life, we created a surprising family ritual that brought us closer together.

[In the] summer [of 2000], 26 million Americans spent their Wednesday nights watching *Survivor* and CBS is hoping version two, which started airing in late January [2001], will do just as well. Our family of five was among the 26 million. For us, the expenditure of those sixty minutes each week was more than buying into a media phenomenon. It was an investment in our family that will pay out long-term dividends.

Using Reality TV to Examine Human Nature

Awareness of "what people are talking about" is a core value my wife and I are committed to teaching our three daughters. The dialect of popular culture is the language our generation speaks. Watching those sixteen castaways on a deserted island in the South China Sea provided our family with a fine way to stay in touch with popular culture. As a Christian minister I must be able to communicate my faith in terms a sight-and-sound generation can understand. The same is true for all followers of the carpenter from Nazareth who told stories his listeners easily identified with. To that end, my wife and I make it a point to stay on top of whatever is "the rage." That would include *Who Wants to Be a Millionaire*, the Academy Award nominees, contemporary hits on the Billboard charts, and of course the daily headlines.

As we watched *Survivor*, my wife, Wendy, and I seized on teachable moments with our girls. The marooned would-be millionaires represented an interesting spectrum of humanity. Vocations, values, and motives were diverse. In addition to the rats and snakes, the ugly monster of greed could easily be seen among the Tagi and Pagong tribes. Talking with our family about the castaways' beliefs and behavior provided an opportunity to talk on what the Bible says about human nature. We discovered that in each person on the island, we could see a reflection of our imperfect selves. We could see the ways we try to manipulate each other to get our own way, the ways we scheme to undermine other family members, the ways our words can hurt people we love.

Gathering around the TV as a family became a Wednesday night ritual at our house. We arranged our hectic sched-

The Redeeming Qualities of Reality TV

The entertainment offered by reality TV lies in separating the aspects of subjects' behavior that are motivated by an awareness of the cameras from the aspects that are genuine. You can't expect someone who's surrounded by cameras to act naturally all of the time, and as the genre has evolved, editors and producers have become aware that highlighting this gap between the real self and the camera-ready self . . . constitutes quality entertainment. . . . When "Big Brother 5's" Jason pouts his lips, flexes his muscles and adjusts his metrosexual headband in the mirror, then confides to the camera that every idiotic thing he's done in the house so far has been part of a master plan to confuse his roommates, he . . . hints at narcissistic and sociopathic streaks that reality TV has demonstrated may be a defining characteristic of the modern personality. Either an alarming number of reality show contestants are self-obsessed and combative, or the common character traits found in young people have shifted dramatically. . . .

When we see Puck of "The Real World" screeching at the top of his lungs or Richard Hatch of "Survivor" confiding to the cameras that he considers the other players beneath him, we may be glimpsing behavior that's more true of the average American than any of us would like to believe. . . .

The process of getting to know the characters, of discovering the qualities and flaws that define them, and then discussing these discoveries with other viewers creates a simulation of community that most people don't find in their everyday lives. . . . These shows unearth a heartfelt desire to make connections with other human beings. Better that we rediscover our interest in other, real people than sink ourselves into the mirage of untouchable celebrity culture or into some überhuman, ultraclever fictional "Friends" universe.

Heather Havrilesky, *Salon*, September 13, 2004.

---

ules around it. Even while visiting with relatives we asked permission to watch "our show." For the last episode of the series, we went all out. All the ficus trees in the house were hauled into the family room, along with a menagerie of stuffed jungle animals (including a four-foot-long snake). A tiki torch, Polynesian trinkets, and a treasure chest surrounded the TV. There was even a Malaysian vase into which we each cast our votes for who we wanted to win. As we watched the two-hour finale, we feasted on steamed rice, barbecue chicken, tropical fruit, and dirt cups—chocolate pudding, crushed Oreo cookies, and gummy worms. In the process of watching *Survivor*, something occurred that I wouldn't have expected. We experienced the kind of family bonding therapists write about. Wendy, Kristin, Allison, Lauren, and I shared a common commitment (even if it was just a TV show). As a result, we prioritized the experience. It became a ritual. The shared ritual caused us to place increased value in each other.

As our closest friends know, our *Survivor* celebration is only one among a continuing pattern of such customized family celebrations. Come World Series time, we'll decorate the fireplace mantle with baseball memorabilia and have a hot-dog dinner complete with Cracker Jacks. Since my wife's roots are north of the border, we annually observe Canadian Thanksgiving in a big way. Our girls' favorite family tradition is our Academy Award party. We dress up in our grandest finery, sit down to a dinner of candlelight and silver and cast our ballots for our favorite nominees before watching the ceremonies together.

Traditions Are Sacred

Rituals and traditions are one of the most underutilized keys to the survival of marriages and families. In the jungle of self-interest, compromise, and competing loyalties, repeated shared experiences remind us of our identity. They also offer a sense of security by which we can face unfamiliar circumstances. No wonder individuals who practice a faith that places a high value on rituals have a lower divorce rate than do those with do-it-yourself belief systems.

Because there is redemptive value in family rituals, even something as pedestrian as watching the same program each week together can be a sacred experience. And that for me is worth more than a million bucks!

*"The message for young female viewers
[is] that . . . if one fails to match the
'thin ideal,' one may be subjected to
sarcasm, derision, [and] ridicule."*

Television Programs Debase Women

Gregory Fouts and Kimberley Burggraf

Gregory Fouts and Kimberley Burggraf are psychology professors at the University of Calgary. In the following viewpoint they declare that television shows degrade and stereotype women. Too often, they charge, male sitcom characters joke about the weight of female characters—the heavier the woman, the more subject to jokes she is. This phenomenon reinforces stereotypes that women must be very thin to be attractive, the authors avow. Even more disconcerting, contend Fouts and Burggraf, audience laughter heard after derisive comments implies that it is appropriate to ridicule women's bodies. Because television teaches that even average-weight women are overweight and unattractive, the authors caution, young female viewers may become dissatisfied with their bodies and develop eating disorders.

As you read, consider the following questions:
1. According to the authors, what do researchers say about the combination of modeling and vicarious verbal reinforcement?
2. Name three reasons it was important to focus on negative comments about heavier women's bodies on television, as cited by Fouts and Burggraf.

Gregory Fouts and Kimberley Burggraf, "Television Situation Comedies: Female Weight, Male Negative Comments, and Audience Reactions," *Sex Roles: A Journal of Research*, May 2000, p. 925. Copyright © 2000 by Plenum Publishing Corporation. Reproduced by permission of the authors.

A content analysis of 18 prime-time television situation comedies (two episodes each) examined the body weights of 37 central female characters (92% White, 8% Black), the negative comments they received from male characters about their weight or bodies, and the audience reactions (e.g., laughter) following the negative comments. It was found that (a) below-average weight females were over-represented in the programs, (b) the heavier the female character, the significantly more negative comments were made about or to her, and (c) negative comments were significantly associated with audience reactions. These results indicate that situation comedies present males making derogatory remarks about heavier women's weights and bodies, with this behavior being reinforced by audience laughter. This combination of thinness modeling and vicarious reinforcement likely contributes to the internalization of gender and weight stereotypes which deleteriously affect the health of female adolescents.

Past Research

Several studies have documented the thinness and attractiveness stereotypes of women presented in television advertising and programming. For example, [Lois] Kaufman reported that few prime-time TV characters (12%) were overweight and underrepresented the proportion of overweight individuals in the general population. [Researchers B.] Silverstein, [L.] Perdue, [B.] Peterson, and [I.] Kelly found that 5% of female TV characters were rated as "heavy," whereas 69% of female characters were rated as "thin." [Gregory] Fouts and [Kimberley] Burggraf recently reported that 33% of central female characters in situation comedies were "below average" in weight, with 60% and 7% being "average" and "above average" in weight, respectively. These studies indicate that the modeling of women's bodies on television is distorted and that this pattern has been consistent for the past 20 years. Exposure to these images likely leads many young women to internalize these images, compare themselves with these images, and form distorted mental constructions of and dissatisfaction with their bodies; some may also exhibit eating disorder symptomatology.

Researchers examining the influence of television on young viewers have argued not only that modeling is a powerful social influence variable, but that the combination of modeling and vicarious verbal reinforcement may be particularly detrimental for viewers. That is, vicarious positive reinforcement and punishment provide viewers with information as to what is and is not acceptable, as well as motivations and inhibitions, respectively, for engaging in modeled behavior. Fouts and Burggraf analyzed television situation comedies and found that the thinner the female character, the more positive comments she received about her body from male characters. They concluded that the message for female viewers is that, in order to be attractive to and receive positive comments from males, one has to be slim; and the message for male viewers is that it is acceptable to make positive comments about women's bodies when they are thin and to withhold these comments from heavier women. They argued that exposure to such differential vicarious verbal reinforcement may contribute to the internalization of the "thin ideal" stereotype in young viewers.

The Importance of Studying Comments About Heavier Female Characters

The purpose of the present study was to extend this research by examining situation comedies and determining (a) the occurrence of negative comments made by males associated with women's bodies and whether such comments are directed toward heavier women, and (b) the occurrence of audience reactions to the negative comments and the relationship between these comments and audience reactions. Situation comedies (e.g., "Friends," "Mad About You") were the target of this study because they are the most popular programs for young adolescents and, thus, are the most likely to influence young viewers during the developmental stage when they are forming their adult body self-concepts. Male comments on television were focused upon because young women often define their physical attractiveness and desirability through their interactions with males who hold gender stereotypes, and past research has found no association between female characters' comments and the body shapes and weights of other female characters.

Negative comments about heavier women's bodies on television were of interest for three reasons. First, observing vicarious punishment (e.g., "Don't you need to lose a few pounds?" "How about wearing a sack!") associated with average or heavier bodies may reinforce negative stereotypes of heavier women (e.g., unattractive, undesirable) in young viewers. Second, such reinforcement may lower the self-esteem of young women who are experiencing normal pubertal changes in their bodies through the internalization of the emotional content of the negative comments. Third, the combination of positive reinforcement for desired behavior and punishment for undesired behavior is considered far more effective in internalizing and altering behavior than either alone. This differential reinforcement associated with body shape/weight is likely presented in television situation comedies. Although positive comments have been associated with degree of thinness of characters, it is important to determine whether negative comments are directed toward women who do not fit the "thin ideal."

Audience Reactions Reflect Society's Views

Audience reactions refer to events which immediately follow the comments and/or behaviors of television actors performing in character. These reactions may come from a live studio audience which is present during the taping, or they may occur by virtue of a tape editor who places bits of prerecorded "laugh tracks" or "canned laughter" onto the final program before it is broadcast. These laugh tracks are professionally produced and offer an editor a variety of audience reactions to fit particular comments and behaviors in the program, e.g., booming laugh of many audience members, "oohs," or only a few audience members reacting. Audience reactions to television characters are important for two reasons. First, an audience may be conceptualized as the societal context in which comments made by individual members of that society are supported. Thus, when negative comments about women's bodies are made by male characters and are followed by audience laughter, this suggests implicit societal approval that heavier women's bodies are laughable and/or to be ridiculed and punished. Second, audience reaction is a type of "reinforcement of reinforcement." That is, hearing audience reactions to negative comments about women's bodies may vicariously reinforce the behavior for viewers, thus increasing the likelihood that they will internalize this behavior and subsequently either use it on and/or accept it from others.

Many Television Sitcoms Are Misogynistic

Young women today seem to believe that all [feminist] battles are won and they can pretty much "be and do whatever they want" without any political effort at all. That's why they are so uncritical of the increasingly woman-centered, but far from feminist, television series they watch, and so oblivious to the contradictions and misogynies that inflect these shows.

When I showed a segment of *Ally McBeal* to a "Gender and Media" class recently it was, remarkably, the male students (forced to deal with these issues for the first time) who were most likely to be shocked at the negative stereotypes. . . . Said [one young man], "These women are so competitive and catty, and so man-crazy.". . . These puzzled young men's remarks were met (to my dismay) with utter contempt by some of the brightest and most outspoken of my women students. . . ."But that's how women really are;" they insisted, or, "That's what you have to do to be successful."

Undeniably there's much truth in these attitudes. Postfeminism has created some very poor role models for women in real life and on television, and Ally McBeal is certainly one of them. . . .

There are the new, terminally soppy, "professional woman" shows like *Providence* and *Judging Amy*, in which successful professional women leave the big city to return to their small town homes and move back in with Mum and Dad to live very rose-tinted, nostalgic versions of 1950s lives. . . .

Women, strong, successful women, are everywhere on television today. But their lives are so devoid of any meaning or purpose, except the most reactionary desires for traditional relationships and families and/or lots of money, that it is as though we have won the battle but lost the war.

Elayne Rapping, *Women's Review of Books*, July 2000.

Since television programs reflect the gender stereotypes and behaviors of the society in which viewers live, we have two predictions: (a) a positive association between weight of female television characters and the receipt of negative comments by male characters, and (b) a positive association between the frequencies of negative comments and audience reactions. Thus, the present study examined two possible vicarious reinforcement/punishment contingencies in situation comedies (negative verbalizations about body weight and audience reactions to these verbalizations) which may promote the learning of gender stereotypes and unhealthy behaviors in young viewers.

Study Methods

Situation comedies are half-hour television programs appearing in prime time (7–11 P.M.); they present comedic plots and/or characters and contain audience reactions (live or taped). Eighteen situation comedies were available in the Calgary [Canada] area (January 26–February 8, 1997). Two episodes of each were recorded. Within these programs, 37 female characters (92% White, 8% Black) were identified as central characters appearing weekly; the actresses for the characters were those consistently listed in the main credits of the program (e.g., for "Friends," Courtney Cox, Lisa Kudrow, and Jennifer Aniston). A total of 74 characters (37 × 2 episodes) was observed and coded. . . .

For descriptive and comparative purposes, the body weight images of central female characters were categorized as "below average weight" (1–3 on [researchers A.E.] Fallon and [P.] Rozin's scale [of body shapes]), "average weight" (4–6), and "above average weight" (7–9). The three scores within each category were assumed to reflect the normal variation of body shapes within the category, with the below- and above-average categories reflecting more extreme scores. These categories were not used by Fallon and Rozin, although similar categorizations have been used by others. Seventy-six percent of the female characters were below average in weight, with 19% and 5% being average and above-average weight, respectively. These percentages are similar to [the 1986 findings] of Silverstein et al., who used a different system for coding the weight of television characters; this similarity in findings suggests consistency in the judgment of body image and/or prevalence rates among television characters over time. The percentage of below-average weight female characters markedly contrasts with the actual prevalence rate of women in society (24%). This finding is consistent with past research which indicates an overrepresentation of below-average weight women in television programs that adolescents watch, thus presenting an unrealistic picture of women's bodies in society.

Harmful Messages for Male and Female Viewers

Fourteen percent of the central female characters received negative comments from males regarding their weight or bodies. A significant correlation was found between the frequency of negative comments and the weight of female characters (using the 9-point scale); i.e., the heavier the female character, the more negative comments she received from male characters. This finding has important implications. The message for young female viewers appears to be that males do pay attention to women's bodies; and if one fails to match the "thin ideal," one may be subjected to sarcasm, derision, ridicule, and "helpful" suggestions to lose weight or how to dress to hide a "weight problem." As a consequence, female viewers who identify with heavier female characters may experience a lowering of self-esteem through experiencing the negative comments themselves. For male viewers, they observe modeling by popular television characters that it is acceptable to comment negatively about (and possibly harass) women who do not fit the "thin ideal" and to respond differentially to women according to their body weights.

Fouts and Burggraf reported that situation comedies show male characters making positive comments to women according to their body weight; i.e., the thinner the woman, the more positive comments she receives. The present study demonstrates the converse, i.e., heavier women receive more negative comments from males. This combination of observing differential positive reinforcement and punishment has been shown to be the most efficient method of teaching values and behavior. Thus, situation comedies provide a training ground for males to learn how to respond differentially to women according to their body weights. Concomitantly, for females, it may establish expectations and perhaps acceptance of these values and behaviors by males.

An examination of audience reactions revealed that 80% of negative comments made by males were followed by audience reactions such as laughter, "oohs," and giggles. A significant correlation was found between the frequency of negative comments a female character received and the frequency of audience reactions; i.e., the greater the number of negative comments characters received, the more frequent the audience reactions. This finding has, at least, four implications. First, the modeling of making negative comments about heavier women results in approval or reinforcement by an audience or group within society; thus, the effect of this modeling may increase due to the vicarious reinforcement it receives. Second, there is modeling by the audience; i.e., it is acceptable to react positively (e.g., with laughter) to instances of hurtful comments directed toward heavier women, even women who are of average weight. Third, the more negative comments are made about women's weight, the greater the reaction (and funnier it is) to others, thus likely encouraging such behavior in the presence of others. Fourth, television situation comedies not only reflect stereotypic values within society, but also model gender stereotypes, e.g., that heavier women are unattractive, undesirable, and laughable.

> *"Young men learn [from television] that they are expected to screw up, that women will have the brains to their brawn, and that child care is over their heads."*

Television Programs Debase Men

Michael Abernathy

Far too many television shows typecast men as inconsiderate, uninvolved with their families, and incapable of performing domestic chores, argues Michael Abernathy in the following viewpoint. In Abernathy's contention, stereotypes of males are just as destructive as stereotypes of women or minorities. Depictions of men as inferior and dependent on their wives undermine the notion of sex equality, he avers, and teach that only women, portrayed as smarter and more competent, can handle childcare and housework. It is disturbing that few positive role models exist on television for young boys, suggests Abernathy. Abernathy is a film and TV critic for PopMatters.com.

As you read, consider the following questions:
1. Which shows feature women who have better qualities than their husbands, in Abernathy's view?
2. According to the author, what were the findings of the Children Now study?
3. What point does the author make about shows such as *Amos and Andy* and *I Dream of Jeannie?*

Michael Abernathy, "Character Flaw; Male-Bashing Has Become Fair Game on TV," *Seven Days* (Burlington, VT), vol. 9, June 9–16, 2004, p. 32A. Copyright © 2004 by *Seven Days*. Reproduced by permission of Popmatters.com.

Warning for our male readers: The following article contains big words and complex sentences. It might be a good idea to have a woman nearby to explain it to you.

It has been a hard day. Your assistant at work is out with the flu and there is another deadline fast approaching. Your wife is at a business conference, so you have to pick up your son at daycare, make dinner, clean the kitchen, do a load of laundry, and get Junior to bed before you can settle down on the sofa with those reports you need to go over.

Perhaps a little comedy will make the work more bearable, you think, so you turn on CBS's Monday night comedies: "Yes, Dear," "Everybody Loves Raymond" and "Still Standing." You'll see three male lead characters who are nothing like you. These men are selfish and lazy, inconsiderate husbands and poor parents.

And the commercials in between aren't any better. Among them, a feminine hygiene ad: Two women are traveling down a lovely country road, laughing and having a great time. But wait. One of them needs to check the freshness of her minipad, and, apparently, the next rest area is six states away. A woman's voice-over interjects, "It's obvious that the Interstate system was designed by men."

A digital-camera ad: A young husband walks through a grocery store, trying to match photos in his hand with items on the shelves. Cut to his wife in the kitchen, snapping digital pictures of all the items in the pantry so that hubby won't screw up the shopping.

A family game ad: A dorky guy and beautiful woman are playing Trivial Pursuit. He asks her, "How much does the average man's brain weigh?" Her answer: "Not much."

Television's Portrayal of Men as Imbeciles

Welcome to the new comic image of men on TV: incompetence at its worst. Where television used to feature wise and wonderful fathers and husbands, today's comedies and ads often feature bumbling husbands and inept, uninvolved fathers. On "Still Standing," Bill (Mark Addy) embarrasses his wife Judy (Jamie Gertz) so badly in front of her reading group, that she is dropped from the group. On "Everybody Loves Raymond," Raymond (Ray Romano) must choose between bathing the twin boys or helping his daughter with her homework. He begrudgingly agrees to assist his daughter, for whom he is no help whatsoever.

CBS is not the only guilty party. ABC's "My Wife and Kids" and "According to Jim," Fox's "The Bernie Mac Show," "The Simpsons," and "Malcolm in the Middle," and the WB's "Reba" also feature women who are better organized and possess better relational skills than their male counterparts. While most television dramas tend to avoid gender stereotypes, as these undermine "realism," comic portrayals of men have become increasingly negative. The trend is so noticeable that it has been criticized by men's rights groups and some television critics.

It has also been studied by academicians Dr. Katherine Young and Paul Nathanson in their book, *Spreading Misandry: The Teaching of Contempt for Men in Popular Culture*. Young and Nathanson argue that in addition to being portrayed as generally unintelligent, men are ridiculed, rejected and physically abused in the media. Such behavior, they suggest, "would never be acceptable if directed at women."

Evidence of this pattern is found in a 2001 survey of 1000 adults conducted by the Advertising Standards Association in Great Britain, which found that two thirds of respondents thought that women featured in advertisements were "intelligent, assertive and caring," while the men were "pathetic and silly." The number of respondents who thought men were depicted as "intelligent" was a paltry 14 percent. (While these figures apply to the United Kingdom, comparable advertisements air in the U.S.)

What's Wrong with Joking About Men?

Some feminists might argue that for decades women on TV looked mindless, and that turnabout is fair play. True, many women characters through the years have had little more to do than look after their families. From the prim housewife whose only means of control over her children was "Wait till your father gets home!" to the dutiful housewife whose husband declares, "My wife: I think I'll keep her," women in the '50s and '60s were often subservient. (This generalization leaves out the unusual exception like Donna Reed, who produced her own show, on which she was not subservient.)

Then, during the "sexual revolution," TV began to feature independent women who could take care of themselves: Mary and Rhoda on "The Mary Tyler Moore Show," Julia, Alice and Flo on "Alice," Louise and Florence on "The Jeffersons." So now, 30 years later, you'd think that maybe we'd have come to some parity. Not even.

Granted, men still dominate television, from the newsroom to prime time. And men do plenty on their own to perpetuate the image of the immature male, from Comedy Central's "The Man Show" to the hordes of drunken college boys who show up every year on MTV's "Spring Break." What's the problem with a few jokes about how dumb men can be? C'mon, can't we take a few jokes?

If only it was just a few. The jokes have become standard fare. Looking at a handful of sitcoms makes the situation seem relatively insignificant, but when those sitcoms are combined with dozens of negative ads which repeat frequently, then a poor image of men is created in the minds of viewers.

Television Perpetuates Damaging Stereotypes

According to "Gender Issues in Advertising Language" [in the book *Women and Language*], television portrayals that help create or reinforce negative stereotypes can lead to problems with self-image, self-concept and personal aspirations. Young men learn that they are expected to screw up, that women will have the brains to their brawn, and that child care is over their heads. And it isn't just men who suffer from this constant parade of dumb men on TV. Children Now reports a new study that found that two thirds of children they surveyed describe men on TV as angry and only one third report ever seeing a man on television performing domestic chores, such as cooking or cleaning. There are far too few positive role models for young boys on television.

Moreover, stereotypical male-bashing portrayals undermine the core belief of the feminist movement: equality. Just think. What if the butt of all the jokes took on another identity? Consider the following fictional exchanges:

"It is so hard to get decent employees." "That's because you keep hiring blacks."

"I just don't understand this project at all." "Well, a woman explained it to you, so what did you expect?"

"I can't believe he is going out again tonight." "Oh, please, all Hispanics care about is sex."

Commentary on a Sitcom That Degrades Men

[The *Roseanne*] sitcom gives us a chance to see a blue-collar feminist. . . . Informed that a wife had stabbed her husband 37 times, Miss [Roseanne] Barr commented: "I admire her restraint." This translates as: "Take my husband—please." The jokes which, when applied to [women], were condemned as crude exploitation of vicious stereotypes, now reappear in cross-dressing to progressive applause. Apparently, it was not the crudity to which the anti-sexists objected . . . but the sexual identity of the original targets. . . . Now it is always men who play the butt. When stickers used to read, "This joke degrades women," the sticker was social criticism; if a sticker were now to state, "This joke degrades men," the social criticism would be the joke.

Jim Atkinson, *National Review*, September 3, 1990.

All of these statements are offensive, and would rightfully be objected to by advocates of fair representation in the media. However, put the word "man" or "men" in place of "blacks," "woman," and "Hispanics" in the above sentences and they're deemed humorous. Are men who ask to be treated civilly overly sensitive or are we as justified in our objections as members of NOW [National Organization for Women], the NAACP [National Association for the Advancement of Colored People], GLAAD [Gay & Lesbian Alliance Against Defamation] and other groups which protest demeaning television portrayals?

Most of the shows I'm talking about are popular. Maybe that means I am being too sensitive. Yet, many U.S. viewers didn't have a problem with "Amos and Andy" or "I Dream of Jeannie," both famous for their offensive stereotypes. These shows enjoyed good ratings, but neither concept is likely to be revived anytime soon, as "society" has realized their inappropriateness.

Fortunately, some people are working to change the way television portrays men. J.C. Penney ran an ad [in 2003] for a One Day sale, with a father at the breakfast table, with his infant crying and throwing things. The father asks the child when his mother will be home. Lana Whited of *The Roanoke Times*, syndicated columnist Dirk Lammers, and the National Men's Resource Center were just a few who objected to this image of an apparently incompetent and uncaring father. Penney's got the message; their later holiday ad features a father, mother, and son all happily shopping together.

Undoubtedly, some men out there are clones of Ward Cleaver, just as some men resemble Al Bundy. But the majority is somewhere in between. We're trying to deal the best we can with the kids, the spouse, the job, the bills, the household chores and the countless crises that pop up unexpectedly. After all that, when we do get the chance to sit down and relax, it would be nice to turn on the TV and not see ourselves reflected as idiots.

"[On reality] dating shows . . . gay men function principally as romantic pariahs, the surprise Old Maid Card hidden in the deck of boy-girl romance, and are not portrayed as desiring beings."

Reality TV Shows Perpetuate Stereotypes of Gays

Dana Stevens

Dana Stevens argues in the following viewpoint that reality TV shows depict homosexuals inaccurately. Gay men, she notes, are never shown dating other men, while lesbians are excluded completely from reality shows. The few reality programs that portray gay relationships do so under a cruel guise, she claims; bachelorettes must determine which of their male suitors are gay by asking them about fashion and culture, reinforcing stereotypes of gay men as stylish and worldly. On these shows, Stevens concludes, gays win only by pretending to be straight. This reflects a larger societal problem, she posits; heterosexuals remain uncomfortable with and are unwilling to acknowledge gay relationships. Stevens writes on television, film, and culture.

As you read, consider the following questions:
1. Where are lesbians found on television and under what conditions, in Stevens's contention?
2. Name three activities that *Playing It Straight* implies are "gay," according to author.
3. In Ciara Byrne's opinion, what was difficult for the gay contestants on *Playing It Straight?*

W hat's going on with gay men and reality television? Even as the debate rages about whether or not to deface the U.S. Constitution with an amendment banning gay marriage, practitioners of the love that dare not speak its name are repainting America's apartments, critiquing our moisturizers, hurling us into black SUVs, and taking us to the barber.

Reality Shows Stereotype Gays

And that's just on Bravo's playful makeover hit *Queer Eye for the Straight Guy*, which has brought gay men into the mainstream, not as subjects or objects of desire, but as dispensers of fashion, taste, and wit. On dating shows like Fox's new *Playing It Straight*—postmillennial versions of *The Price Is Right*, where what you win is no longer a 30-foot catamaran but a fortune, a lifestyle, and a mate—gay men have come to serve a different function, something between booby prize and bargaining chip; they're what's behind curtain No. 3. It might be said that by complicating the binary logic of the heterosexual dating show, gay men have earned themselves a tenuous perch on television, but at what cost? The one thing that gay men still can't be found doing on reality television is the very thing that defines them as "gay" in the first place: loving other men.

Whether overhauling the straight guy's wardrobe or flirting with his potential girlfriend, gay men on reality television exist to impart some intangible quality of sophistication or savoir-faire to the otherwise drab lives of their heterosexual brothers. In their more positive *Queer Eye* incarnation, they're allowed to be arbiters of style, smartass sidekicks, sexually non-threatening superheroes on a mission from Planet Fabulous. In the more depressing . . . world of dating shows like *Playing It Straight*, gay men function principally as romantic pariahs, the surprise Old Maid Card hidden in the deck of boy-girl romance, and are not portrayed as desiring beings. (As for lesbians, they have been conspicuously absent from the reality-TV scene. Perhaps that's because, ever since Ellen DeGeneres' legendary on-air coming out in 1997, lesbians seem to have carved themselves a cozy primetime niche in which they can love other ladies with impunity,

as long as everyone concerned is affluent, extraordinarily attractive, and most important, fictional—see Showtime's new
Sapphic soap opera *The L Word.*)

Cruel Tricks with Harmful Consequences

Last summer's *Boy Meets Boy* (Bravo) at first presented itself
as a gay version of *The Bachelor*, with a charming young catch
named James whittling his way through a field of 15 prospective boyfriends. But midway through the season, James, along
with the viewing audience, discovered that a cruel trick had
been played on him: Of the three remaining men, only two
shared his sexual orientation. (In a rare moment of reality-
TV candor, James' straight female friend Andra lost it when
she found out about the producers' deception, screaming
"This is BULLSHIT!" and encouraging him to leave the
show. Instead, James stayed, ended up choosing one of the
gay men, and won them both a trip to New Zealand.)

Boy Meets Boy was stupid, mean-spirited, and shallow, but
Fox's new series *Playing It Straight*, the first gay-themed reality show to appear on network television, wins the race to
the bottom. The setup: Jackie, identified by the voice-over
narrator as an "innocent young girl" with "small-town values," is isolated on a Nevada ranch with 14 strapping lads.
Over the course of the season, she will choose a mate in traditional reality-show fashion, by eliminating two contenders
per episode through a series of talking-head interviews and
horribly uncomfortable televised picnics. The twist, revealed
to Jackie in the season opener, is that an undisclosed number
of these suitors are, in actuality, batting left-handed. They're
polishing with, not against, the grain of wood. They're . . .
well, you know. That way. Seriously, I would rather listen to
the euphemistic prevarications of a Tennessee Williams
heroine than sit again through the montage from the open-
ing episode of *Playing It Straight*, in which a lineup of ner-
vous, defensive contestants confesses to the enjoyment of
such questionably gendered activities as baking a cheesecake,
using a hair dryer, and "singing Spanish ballads." (My favorite is the guy who sheepishly concedes, "I do know a *little* bit about art." Good luck, gallery boy!)

Watching *Playing It Straight* is a gender theorist's day in the sun. . . . Let's look at the show's two prospective outcomes. If Jackie guesses "right" and narrows the field down to a straight man, then the two of them will split the $1 million prize and ride off into the sunset in a chauffeured car, glasses of champagne awkwardly balanced on their laps. But if one of the secretly gay men tricks her into choosing him, he will walk off with a cool million all his own. In other words, "Sizzling Saddles Ranch" (an Elko, Nev., resort that was thus mortifyingly renamed by the show's producers) is a microcosm of American society, where gays can best get ahead by remaining alone in the closet while straights openly pair-bond and consolidate their resources.

Reality TV Promotes Harmful Stereotypes of Gays

[One reality show featured] two straight men competing for a $50,000 prize by trying to fool people—including their close friends—into thinking they're gay. It was an exercise in systematic humiliation, with contestants who referred to the experience on-camera as their "worst nightmare" and who bemoaned that they were "trapped in gay hell.". . . [Besides performing embarassing stunts, one contestant] had to tell a former teammate that he liked wrestling because he enjoys "close contact with sweaty boys.". . . In exploiting . . . salacious, homophobic stereotypes, [the show's producers] . . . put real gay people in harm's way.

Stephen Macias, "Shooting Straight on Reality TV," *Variety*, June 1, 2004.

What's saddest about shows like *Playing It Straight* is their cheerfully apolitical disavowal of the actual lives of gay people, their staging of a context-free erotic competition that is utterly disconnected from any—dare I say it?—reality outside the gates of Sizzling Saddles. Jackie may hail from a town in Wisconsin too small to have a gay subculture, but many of the male contestants come from cities like Seattle, San Francisco, and Chicago. Straight or gay, can we let these men get away with pretending to think that queerness is signified by hair dryers and cheesecake? It's easy to write off these shows' individual participants as so many gay Uncle Toms [subservient blacks], ready to sell out their sexual identity for a buck, and it's just as easy to turn off the television. (In fact, it was hard to leave it on for the length of time required to re-search this piece since not only is *Playing It Straight* ideolog-ically offensive, it's also colossally boring.) But the hothouse machinations of these psychosexual parlor games have real consequences, not just for the individual participants' lives—in the course of the filming of *Boy Meets Boy*, one of James' suitors, a Navy combat instructor, was discharged after eight years of military service when a fellow sailor spotted him on television—but for the culture as a whole.

The Larger Implications of Gay-Themed Reality Shows

Here's my diagnosis: Shows like *Playing It Straight* are a symp-tom of heterosexual America's collective guilt, our sense as a culture that we are not, in fact, playing straight with the gay community. This guilt is not far from the surface in the hedg-ings of *Playing It Straight*'s executive producer Ciara Byrne in an interview: "Is it fair, is it cool? I'm not sure. . . . I'll be hon-est, some of them found it very difficult, but the upside to that, if there is an upside, is that a lot of them said they came on the show to break stereotypes. . . . Some of them say that this was a very difficult experience, that it felt like being back in the closet. And coming out in America and being gay in America is a very difficult thing, and I think it's an important message for America." The moral confusion and intellectual dishonesty of this statement find their echo in rhetoric from fence-straddlers on both left and right about the future of gay marriage. Reality television, it seems, is like everyday life in at least one sense: The experience of those Americans who love others of their own sex has no real place in it.

"[Reality TV] programs are breaking
fresh ground for gay visibility and defusing
. . . the frustration felt by [gay] activists."

Reality TV Shows Help Debunk Stereotypes of Gays

Erik Meers

In the following viewpoint Erik Meers, managing editor of *Harper's Bazaar*, credits reality TV with helping to dispel stereotypes of gays. While he concedes that some gay men on reality shows are pigeonholed as flamboyant, he argues that many others are portrayed as real people who do not always fit that stereotype. Furthermore, Meers points out, gay reality show participants help to publicize issues that affect gays, from AIDS to the military's "don't ask, don't tell" policy, which allows gays to serve so long as they do not disclose their homosexuality. He asserts that reality shows humanize lesbian and gay relationships in a way that fictional television programs cannot.

As you read, consider the following questions:

1. In Meers's view, how do gay reality show participants differ from Will in *Will & Grace?*
2. How does the author explain the fact that there are more Brandons and fewer Wills on reality TV?
3. According to Meers, why didn't people consider Richard Hatch a role model for gays?

Erik Meers, "Keeping It Real; Gays and Lesbians Are Everywhere in Life, So of Course They're on Reality TV. From Lance Loud to Chris Beckman and Brandon Quinton, the Diverse Bunch of Out Gays on These Shows Brings Viewers Face-to-Face with Our Queer Lives," *Advocate*, April 30, 2002, p. 38. Copyright © 2002 by Liberation Publications, Inc. Reproduced by permission.

Lesbians and gays are everywhere on the tube this spring [2002] courtesy of the endless proliferation of reality TV. In addition to [homosexuals Chris Beckman and Aneesa on] *The Real World*, the CBS juggernaut *Survivor: Marquesas* features out castaway John Carroll, a nurse from Omaha [Nebraska] as well as a rumored lesbian yet to be revealed, and *The Amazing Race 2* highlights gay buddies Oswald and Danny from Miami. This fall, *Eco-Challenge Fiji 2002*—a grueling 500-plus-kilometer race to be broadcast on the USA Network—will feature on all-gay team sponsored by Subaru. And this is not to mention the countless openly gay people who continue to pop up as participants everywhere, including *Who Wants to Be a Millionaire*, the various confront-your-fears shows, and possibly even that heterofest *Temptation Island*.

Reality Shows Benefit Homosexuals

All these vérité programs are breaking fresh ground for gay visibility and defusing a bit of the frustration felt by activists at the timidity of some fictional network shows like *Will & Grace*. "Five seasons ago on *The Real World*, we would not see someone like [Beckman] lying in bed and kissing his boyfriend. It's wonderful. There's nothing salacious about it," says Scott Seomin, entertainment media director for the Gay and Lesbian Alliance Against Defamation [GLAAD]. "*Will & Grace* is a great show, and it has done an amazing amount for our community, but it's a hit because it conforms to the sitcom format to make the majority of this country comfortable. We have seen Grace making lots of passionate noises with her boyfriend. We have not seen that with Will."

Unlike the sex-starved Will, Chris and Aneesa date, cuddle, and sleep with their same-sex love interests. And unlike the heated romances of *ER*'s Dr. Kerry Weaver or the "questioning" youth story lines on *Boston Public* and *Once and Again*, their doings can't be dismissed as ratings-driven character development. In a recent episode of *The Real World*, for example, when Aneesa ripped into her game-playing girlfriend for bringing her ex by the apartment, the tears and expletives flowed from immediate emotions, not from a writer's pen.

"It was real," recalls Aneesa. "I was upset and I was mad. I wish I wouldn't have cursed as much. I gave [the producers] everything. I kept one or two things private, but everything else is out there. I would be so embarrassed to go home and have people say, 'Aneesa, that is not you.' Aneesa does not hold back one ounce of her personality.

"I cried more there than I have in the last five years," she continues. "It was therapy for me. We all make mistakes—and I get to see mine every week." While many will shake their heads at Aneesa's antics, most can relate to her frustration with an unresponsive lover. Such scenes humanize gay relationships to an impressionable audience in a way that fictional shows can't.

Portraying Gays as "Gay"

Survivor: Africa's Brandon Quinton can probably advise Aneesa on living with an over-the-top TV persona. "I knew they were going to play me up to be really flamboyant," Quinton says of his portrayal on the show. "They made us all extreme. I'm a real person. It wasn't Brandon playing someone else. They edited me extremely, but it was still me."

But by playing into a gay stereotype, *Survivor*'s producers may have made Quinton an easier target for homophobes. He confesses that he no longer reads the mail forwarded to him from the network since almost 10% of it is hate mail. "I just don't want that 'die-fag-die' stuff in my house," he says.

Many gay viewers also bristled at Quinton's campiness. Some even wrote to GLAAD to complain. "I got a lot of E-mail and calls about Brandon," recalls Seomin. "What am I supposed to do, remove him from the show? He's part of the gay community, and we should be embracing him. It was their own internalized homophobia—the fact that he wasn't hypermasculine and had some 'Mary moments,' as I call them. These people E-mailing me are out with their friends calling them 'Mary.' But there is so much shame about who sees that. If we want people to understand our lives, we can't cherry-pick what they see."

Gays on Reality TV Are Breaking Through Stereotypes

In its own subversive way, reality TV is challenging the notion that every gay man on ad-supported TV has to be either

Time Line: The Visibility of Homosexuals on Reality TV

1992 *May: The Real World* premieres on MTV with out cast member Norman Korpi.

1994 *June: The Real World*'s third series features Pedro Zamora, a gay activist with AIDS. During the series Pedro marries his lover, Sean.

November: Zamora dies of AIDS complications, President [Bill] Clinton makes special note of his passing.

1999 *June: The Real World*'s Hawaii season includes both gay law student Justin Deabler and bisexual drama magnet Ruthie Alcaide. . . .

2000 *June:* Danny Roberts stirs up some intrigue with his unidentified military boyfriend in the New Orleans chapter of *The Real World.*

Bravo airs *Fire Island*, a look at two summerhouse shares in the popular resort—one gay, the other lesbian.

August: Openly gay student Brad Krefman is among the students highlighted in the Fox documentary series *American High.* . . .

[Gay contestant Richard] Hatch wins the *Survivor* million-dollar prize in a highly rated final episode.

2001 *January:* ABC's reality game show *The Mole* boasts two gay cast members: Jim Morrison, a lawyer and helicopter pilot, and Jennifer Biondi, a field communications officer.

June: Bravo airs *Gay Riviera*, documenting the lives of several gays and lesbians on the East Coast.

July: In its 10th season, MTV's *Road Rules* adds its first gay contestant, Sophia Pasquis.

CBS's *Big Brother 2* follows suit with gay competitor Bill "Bunky" Miller.

September: CBS and NBC go head-to-head with *The Amazing Race* and *Lost*, both with gay players.

November: Fox's *Temptation Island 2* features Tony Florida as one of the hunks hired to tempt couples into infidelity. Tabloids reveal he was once a performer in a gay-targeted pornographic video. . . .

2002 *March:* HBO's *Taxicab Confessions 2002* debuts with a real-life lesbian marriage in the back of a Las Vegas cab and a lengthy confession from a 20-year-old gay man on his way to a sex club.

Erik Meers, *Advocate*, April 30, 2002.

"straight-acting" or a nonthreatening clown. With each new out reality player, the palette of familiar "gay types" is gradually expanding, whether that means a gay mathematician who gets a Bette Midler question wrong on *Millionaire*, a tough lesbian *Road Rules* contestant who's also one of the show's lookers, or a sensitive gay man on *Big Brother* who loves both his Southern home and his long-term partner.

Preferring larger-than-life participants who will quickly stand out, reality TV by its very nature favors more Brandons and fewer Wills. It has been that way since the beginning: Lance Loud's coming-out on the granddaddy of reality TV shows, 1973's *An American Family*, was politically incorrect long before that phrase existed. Loud lived up to his name, and his determination to find his gay self contributed to the messiness that overtook his family during the filming. Nineteen years later, the creators of *The Real World* took that lesson to heart, adding the openly gay Norm to the first season's cast. The show caught the imagination of the MTV generation and became an instant institution, queer characters and all.

On the second season, Beth Anthony piqued housemates with her aggressively out manner. Looking back now, Anthony says gay visibility was especially vital during the early '90s, before TV stars like Ellen DeGeneres or Rosie O'Donnell came out. "I've had a lot of people come up to me on the street and say that it changed their lives, that their parents understand a little better, that they were in really shaky places and I helped," she says. "Visibility makes a huge difference. I've had thousands of people tell me that." Anthony, who now lives in Los Angeles with her partner of 10 years, Becks, and their 3-year-old daughter, has put that philosophy into practice with her own T-shirt company, featuring both humorous and earnest gay-related designs.

Bringing Gay Issues to the Forefront

Since Norm and Beth, *The Real World* has presented a parade of warm and colorful out personalities, including person-with-AIDS Pedro Zamora in San Francisco; binge-drinker Ruthie in Hawaii; and, in New Orleans, boy-next-door Danny, who dated an enlisted man during the filming, dramatizing the problems with the Pentagon's "don't ask, don't tell" policy.

"The very idea of *The Real World* when we pitched it to MTV in 1992 was putting seven diverse people into a house," observes Jonathan Murray, the show's cocreator. "It almost requires having a gay or lesbian just as it requires having a black or Latino person."

The reality genre took a giant step toward the mainstream with the howling success of the first season of *Survivor* on CBS in summer 2000. Unlike broadcast sitcoms and dramas, where network suits psychoanalyze the import of each character's persona down to their haircut, reality TV seems to have dodged a major-network hurdle—execs' fear of risk taking—an advantage guaranteed by the victory of first *Survivor* winner Richard Hatch.

With his smirking egotism, bearish build, and preference for nudity, Hatch was no one's idea of a gay role model, much less a network superstar. But his soap-operatic connivings were the best thing for CBS's ratings since J.R. Ewing [of *Dallas*]. "I think that Richard Hatch was so popular because of his scheming," observes Julie Salamon, a TV critic for *The New York Times*. "The fact of his being openly gay became important but incidental. In a lot of ways reality shows have been searching for the next Richard Hatch ever since. Having a gay person in the cast is just part of the formula now."

The Gays and Lesbians Next Door

Since the broadcast networks reach a far larger—and more conservative—audience than MTV, the potential social impact of gay people being on major-network shows is profound indeed. After all, reality shows purport to depict reality, so the inclusion of a diverse assortment of gay, lesbian, and bisexual people sends viewers the message that such people are just another variation on who might move in next door. "There's more of a realization that this is part of the population, and it's not a monolithic group of people," says Salamon. "Even in the stupidest situations, that's got to be positive. I think that familiarity breeds indifference—which is a good thing, in this case."

How the queer folks interact with all the straight players simply becomes part of each show's drama. "What I love about it is you don't control the story lines," says *The Real World*'s Murray. "If you have the courage to put a gay or lesbian person on, then you have to be courageous enough to air wherever it takes you. The audience doesn't have as big a problem with it because they know you haven't made those choices as a network. It's happened and you're just showing it. Reality gives the network a license to go into things that ordinarily they might not go into."

With gays popping up all over the cable box, Salamon argues that reality TV has become an easy out for the networks. "Certainly, 10 years ago [having gay people on TV] was something to be commented on," says Salamon. "Now it has become less and less startling. The difference with the people on reality shows [as opposed to fictional series] is that they are there for a short time. On a lot of them, they are kicked off week by week. With something like an *Ellen*, these are characters who are presumably going to be coming into people's homes, in the best case, for years. I don't think this [inclusion] shows a bravery on the part of the reality people. I think it's a different phenomenon."

And sometimes it's something a bit stronger. Over the past decade, the gay housemates on *The Real World* have proved to be among the most popular with viewers. "Danny, without a doubt, got more fan mail than anyone else [that season] and just as much from guys as girls," says Murray. "Not long ago I was with the new cast, and when Chris got up, the audience went crazy." Slowly, a new pantheon of demicelebrities is emerging—one with no need for closets, since their lives, including their sex lives, are televised weekly.

The First Gay Couple on Reality TV

Many gay reality veterans say they've benefited from a kind of homo affirmative action. Life partners Bill Bartek and Joe Baldassare believed as much when applying for the first installment of *The Amazing Race*, a show that follows 11 two-person teams as they sprint around the world chasing a million-dolar prize and getting eliminated one by one. "We thought that [being gay] was our ticket to fortune if we could promote ourselves as a long-term gay couple," says Bartek.

Because the teams consist of people who are already close, *The Amazing Race* "is a relationship show, not just a scavenger hunt," says Bartek, who's been with Baldassare 15 years. "And as far as we knew, there hadn't been a gay couple [on reality TV]. That was the risk we took going into the whole thing, that it was too groundbreaking. We were told by one of the staff members about halfway through the interview process that we were the most stable relationship he'd seen in about 10 years—gay or straight—and [he said,] 'If CBS decides to have enough courage to put on a gay couple, then essentially you guys are on the program.'" CBS bit, and Bartek and Baldassare—who dubbed themselves Team Guido after their pet Chihuahua—came in third on the show.

Periodical Bibliography

The following articles have been selected to supplement the diverse views presented in this chapter.

Craig A. Anderson and Brad J. Bushman
"The Effects of Media Violence on Society," *Science*, March 29, 2002.

Jon Barrett
"The Accidental Activist," *Advocate*, July 18, 2000.

Jane D. Brown
"Mass Media Influences on Sexuality," *Journal of Sex Research*, February 2002.

Free Expression Network
"An Appeal to Reason." www.freeexpression.org.

Michael Freeman
"Women Rise to Power in Upcoming Series," *Electronic Media*, March 19, 2001.

Virginia Heffernan
"Shuttling Stereotypes, a Reality Show Stars Blacks," *New York Times*, January 28, 2004.

Todd Hertz
"Is That You? Perfect Looks, Perfect Hair, Perfect Plot, Perfect Ending. Are These Hollywood Teens Anywhere Close to the Real You?" *Campus Life*, January/February 2004.

Michael Higgins
"Where's Religion on Mainstream TV?" *Toronto Star*, January 15, 2005.

Daphne Lavers
"Media Violence: Ugly and Getting Uglier," *World & I*, March 2002.

Mark Lawson
"Taking Out the Trash: The Backlash Against Reality TV Is Gathering Global Momentum," *Guardian*, March 6, 2004.

Stephen Macias
"Shooting Straight on Reality TV," *Variety*, June 1, 2004.

Elayne Rapping
"You've Come Which Way, Baby?" *Women's Review of Books*, July 2000.

Howard Rosenberg
"Pain, Suffering, Prime Time: For Some, Reality Isn't a TV Show," *Broadcasting & Cable*, November 29, 2004.

Jacob Sullum
"Missing Link," *Reason*, January 23, 2001.

Ray Waddle
"Reality TV: Guilty Pleasure or Window to Our Souls?" United Methodist News Service. www.umc.org.

Steve Weinstein
"Paging Derek Zoolander!" *New York Blade*, October 22, 2004.

CHAPTER 2

What Are Television's Effects on Society?

Chapter Preface

Airing on nearly every channel from PBS to SciFi, reality-based TV programs entertain, annoy, shock, and inspire millions of Americans. Reality shows also generate vociferous debate. Whereas some commentators maintain that reality TV merely reflects the ideals and behaviors of average people, others charge that the programs convince audiences that it is normal and acceptable to humiliate others, betray friends, and engage in other questionable behaviors. The controversy over what effect reality shows may have on Americans is one of many that arise when examining television's influence on society.

According to critics, an especially injurious type of reality program is the makeover show, which they believe perverts society's definitions of beauty and happiness. On *The Swan*, women who dislike their appearance are reconstructed using breast implants, liposuction, face lifts, and whatever other procedures plastic surgeons deem necessary. Afterward, judges determine which "ugly duckling" transitioned into the best swan, hence the show's name. People who protest makeover shows claim that they teach that self-worth and happiness are based on looks and that women who do not fit standard definitions of beauty are perceived as unattractive. TV critic Heather Havrilesky comments that *The Swan* is "freakishly dehumanizing."

Also under fire are reality programs that trick participants, such as *My Big Fat Obnoxious Boss*. The Fox network says of its show, "The con is on! Twelve Ivy League hot shots will humiliate and embarrass themselves . . . competing for a dream job that doesn't exist!" Critics accuse this kind of reality show of exploiting people for the audience's amusement. Reviewer Brian Lowry avows that these programs "hinge on an emotionally detached viewer's willingness to laugh at—and feel superior to—the hapless losers and dupes."

Other cynics denounce reality shows such as *Survivor* in which contestants befriend and then deceive their companions in order to win. Observing this type of behavior week after week has deleterious effects on viewers, according to theology professor Diana L. Hayes. She asserts, "The people of the United States are being bombarded with shows that turn us into opportunistic voyeurs bereft of any sense of morality, compassion, or common decency. Slowly, our sense of outrage is anesthetized." Believing that reality TV is out of touch with the real world, Hayes adds, "If we watch television regularly, we should begin to wonder what the media are trying to convince us of—that this is the way the world is today?"

Interestingly, many fans contend that Americans do in fact act and think much like the people depicted on reality shows. Furthermore, proponents of reality shows suggest, these programs sometimes benefit participants. In "Life After The Swan," former contestants and their families detail the life changes they experienced after the women's makeovers. One contestant's husband declares, "The show made our family stronger." Another participant credits the show's therapist for her self-improvements: "Until the show, I never thought there was something like a doctor checkup for your feelings. I learned to let go of negative things that people say."

Reality programs may contribute to positive changes in attitude as well, maintains Chuck Klosterman of *Spin*. Viewers tend to compare their lives to those on screen, he notes. He discusses the impact this has on society's understanding of what is or is not normal:

> Every family in America—if cast in the context of a reality program—would come across as abnormal. . . . There will be a day when this era of TV is remembered as groundbreaking and vital, because [reality] shows . . . will have destroyed the myth of normalcy. Reality TV will ultimately prove that there is no "normal" way to live, and it will validate the notion that every human experience is autonomous.

Yet another lesson can be learned from reality programming, its supporters aver. In countering assertions that the shows exploit contestants, media analyst James Poniewozik contends, "Embarrassment, these shows demonstrate, is survivable, even ignorable, and ignoring embarrassment is a skill we all could use. It is what you risk—like injury in a sport—in order to triumph."

Reality TV's impact on society is just one topic examined in the following chapter, in which authors explore the extent of television's influence on viewers. Regardless of whether reality shows are found to have a positive or negative effect on audiences, millions of fans will likely continue to tune in.

"By supplanting [children's] imaginations, creating fast-paced pictures, and transforming active minds into passive recipients, TV teaches mental lethargy."

Television Harms Children

Ann Vorisek White

According to Ann Vorisek White in the following viewpoint, television harms the development of young children. To support her claim that children's intellectual, emotional, and moral development is hindered by watching television, she points to findings that the more television youths watch, the weaker their language skills and imaginations. Calling television "an addiction," White criticizes the medium for making kids unresponsive, nonverbal, and dependent on adult supervision. Ann Vorisek White is a children's librarian in Litchfield County, Connecticut.

As you read, consider the following questions:
1. In White's contention, who now parents children?
2. What are the American Academy of Pediatrics's recommendations for childhood TV viewing, according to the author?
3. How does television create dependent children, in White's view?

Ann Vorisek White, "Breaking Out of the Box. Turn Off TV. Turn On Life," *Mothering*, July/August 2001, p. 70. Copyright © 2001 by Mothering Magazine. Reproduced by permission.

The average American child watches four hours of television every day, according to the American Academy of Pediatrics. Videotapes and video games add to the amount of time children spend staring at a screen. How does all this viewing affect us?

Life Before TV

Television harms our children and families in many ways. Before TV, meals were a time for families to reflect upon the day and linger in peace or [for] lively discussion over home-cooked meals. Today, most American families regularly watch television during dinner. Mealtimes are hurried, with children and adults eating in silence, eyes glued to the screen, or gobbling down their food in order to return to the family room to resume their interrupted television watching.

Childhood illnesses and injuries leading to bed rest used to be special times for bonding and family rituals. We can recall books that were read to us or quiet games that we played while recovering from chicken pox or a broken leg. Today, sick children spend their days watching videos and television.

In the past, holiday gatherings found children playing outdoors and adults gathered in lively discussions. Today, children are more apt to gather around the television or computer than to take up a game of kick-the-can or capture-the-flag. In fact, some family gatherings seem to revolve around TV, with Thanksgiving dinners prepared to suit the timing of football games.

Television's Harmful Influence

As a result of the many hours they spend in front of the TV, children are in effect being parented by network producers rather than by their own parents. Television teaches children that rude, irresponsible behavior is not only acceptable but also glamorous. Children learn about sex and violence apart from their consequences, emotional attachments, and responsibilities. They learn to act impulsively, without reflection or advice from elders. Qualities such as wisdom and processes like thinking through a problem are difficult to express on a television screen, especially when the medium depends on sensationalism and shock rather than character and insight.

US Surgeon General David Satcher stated in a 2000 report on youth violence that violent television programming and video games have become a public-health issue and that "repeated exposure to violent entertainment during early childhood causes more aggressive behavior throughout a child's life." The American Psychological Association (APA) notes that children who regularly watch violence on television are more fearful and distrustful of the world, less bothered by violence, and slower to intervene or call for help when they see fighting or destructive behavior. A *Los Angeles Times* story reported that 91 percent of children polled said they felt "upset" or "scared" by violence on television. A University of Pennsylvania study found that children's TV shows contain roughly 20 acts of violence each hour. After watching violent programs, the APA reports, children are more likely to act out aggressively, and children who are regularly exposed to violent programming show a greater tendency toward hitting, arguing, leaving tasks unfinished, and impatience.

Cognitive Development

The first two years of life is when the greatest and most rapid development of the brain occurs. As all parents know, a child's mind is different from an adult's, and the differences go beyond children's innocent and often poetic perceptions of the world. While the adult brain has two distinct hemispheres, the infant brain is a single receptacle of sensory experience in which neither side has developed or overpowered the other. Until they learn language, children absorb experience using a kind of nonverbal "thinking," characterized later in the brain's development as a right hemispheric function. When language begins, each hemisphere seems to be equally developed. In its structural and biochemical sense, the brain doesn't reach its full maturation until about age 12.

By maturation, the left hemisphere typically develops as the dominant side, controlling the verbal and logical functions of the brain, while the right hemisphere controls spatial and visual functions. For many years, such development was thought to be genetically predetermined and unaffected by life experiences. Today, however, this belief has changed. Although the acquisition of language appears to be universal, we now recognize that the abilities required for expression and reasoning are not automatic. Watching television threatens the development of these abilities because it requires a suspension of active cognition.

Television Takes a Toll on Youth

It's hard to understand the world of early adolescents without considering the huge impact on their lives of the mass media. It competes with families, friends, schools and communities in its ability to shape young teens' interests, attitudes and values. . . .

The problem is that young adolescents often don't—or can't —distinguish between what's good in the media and what's bad. Some spend hours in front of the TV or plugged into earphones, passively taking in what they see and hear—violence, sex, profanities, gender stereotyping, and story lines and characters that are unrealistic. . . .

Students who report watching the most TV have lower grades and lower test scores than do those who watch less TV. "In any classroom discussion I have, it is very apparent who's watching [a lot of] television and who's not," explains teacher Sherry Tipps. "For the kids who are not motivated in the classroom, mention TV and suddenly they perk up."

As young teens mature, high levels of TV viewing, video-game playing and computer use take their toll. On average, American children spend far more time with the media than they do completing work for school. Seventh graders, for example, spend an average of 135 minutes each day watching TV and 57 minutes doing schoolwork.

U.S. Department of Education, "Media—Helping Your Child Through Early Adolescence." www.ed.gov.

The American Academy of Pediatrics recommends that children under the age of two not watch TV or videos, and that older children watch only one to two hours per day of nonviolent, educational TV. Young children watching TV are routinely described as transfixed, passive, and nonverbal. One of television's appeals for parents is that it serves as an immediate way to silence and sedate active toddlers. But such nonverbal absorption does more than simply relax and amuse preschoolers. Language spoken by actors on TV does not have the same effect as real-life language experiences. The

Journal of Broadcasting reported that language skills among American children declined as TV viewing time increased.

In real life, conversation is reciprocal and participatory; it allows time for reflection, questions, and encouragement. Television, however, is a one-way street, and you had better stay glued, ask no questions, and take no time for thought, because the next scene will appear in seconds and there is no rewind. As a result, children learn not to think but to remain passive and unresponsive to whatever stimulus appears before them. Television conditions them to absorb images without mental effort and to expect rapid change. Since young children's questions and imaginations are the cornerstone of their learning processes, remaining unresponsive hour after hour, day after day, year after year surely affects their intellectual, emotional, and moral development.

Television Suppresses the Imagination

Fantasy play, a critical component of childhood, allows children to explore different situations with varying responses and outcomes. While books and storytelling nourish fantasy play, fantasy watching does not foster the same reaction. The US Department of Education reported that 81 percent of children ages two to seven watch TV unsupervised, which means that young children enter a world of fantasy without the guidance and oversight of an adult. Research by the Yale University Family Television and Consultation Center reveals that imagination decreases as TV watching increases. TV teaches children to be amused by its images instead of encouraging kids to create their own. It dulls the mind by the power of its fast-moving pictures, supplanting the mental activity necessary to follow in the mind's eye a book or a storyteller's tale. The Yale Center reports that complex language and grammar skills are directly linked to fantasy play, and that children who create fantasy play are more tolerant, peaceful, patient, and happy.

Many children become habituated to TV by their parents, who desire a break from their child's activity and attention. However, the short-term benefit of a quiet, mesmerized child may actually lead to a greater dependence on adult supervision by creating children who are less capable of amusing themselves. By supplanting their imaginations, creating fast-paced pictures, and transforming active minds into passive recipients, TV teaches mental lethargy. For a child raised on hourly doses of TV, boredom is a common component of later childhood. In refusing to use TV during the preschool years, parents may save themselves from constantly having to create amusements for their children.

Healthy Alternate Activities

The best way to keep TV from becoming an issue with children, of course, is not to begin using it. If a TV is present in the home, it is vital to establish clear rules on its use and to maintain these rules. Never make TV a reward or a punishment; this only heightens its power. When starting the withdrawal from TV, explain why you are making these changes and that it is not a punishment. The first month will be the most difficult. Children may cry or plead, but you can remain firm if you keep in mind that you are freeing them from an addiction.

It is also imperative that you help your children learn how to fill the time that they formerly spent watching TV. Work with them to nurture interests, discover hobbies, and explore new possibilities. Begin a nightly read-aloud for the entire family. Take walks after breakfast or dinner. Share your hobbies—sewing, knitting, baking bread—with them. Learn to play instruments and make music as a family. Encourage children to help with work around the house and yard. Visit neighbors and relatives. Tell stories and pass on your family history. Build a birdhouse. Go bowling. Go sledding. Finger paint. Color. Practice yoga together. Involve your children in the daily activities of the house, and encourage yourself and your family to rekindle the flame of exploration and discovery, away from the draw of the flickering blue screen.

"*Television viewing is a much more
intellectual activity for kids than anybody
had previously supposed.*"

Why TV Is Good for Kids

Daniel McGinn

Some television programming can be intellectually stimulating and beneficial to children, argues Daniel McGinn in the following viewpoint. While he admits that much TV programming lacks value, McGinn declares that more quality television shows are broadcast now than ever before. Educational shows, he claims, employ psychologists and other experts to help develop episodes that strengthen children's problem-solving abilities, spatial skills, and vocabulary. Furthermore, claims McGinn, research on children's TV viewing habits has proven that even young children can recall information from television, making it a useful medium for learning. McGinn is a national correspondent for *Newsweek*.

As you read, consider the following questions:

1. What does the author say prompted Daniel Anderson to research children's attention spans during TV viewing?
2. According to McGinn, Colleen Breitbord sees educational programming as so vital to her children's development that she did what?
3. How do *Sesame Street*, *Dragon Tales*, and *Between the Lions* benefit children, according to summative research by PBS?

When Alicia Large was growing up, her parents rarely let her watch television. Even the Muppets were off-limits, she says, because her parents disliked the sexual tension between Kermit and Miss Piggy. Now 31 and raising her own sons—ages 2 and 3—Large views TV more benevolently. Her boys love "Dora the Explorer," so when she takes them on errands, she draws a map—the bank, the grocery store—so they can track their progress as Dora does. Among Large's friends, kids' TV—what and how much are yours watching?—is a constant conversation. Yes, many parents still use TV as a babysitter. But increasingly, she says, parents are looking to TV to help them do a better job of raising kids. "Our generation is using it completely differently," she says.

Parents have felt conflicted about television since its earliest days. Even Philo T. Farnsworth, TV's inventor, fretted over letting his son watch cowboy shows, according to biographer Evan I. Schwartz. That anxiety continues. In a survey released last week by Public Agenda, 22 percent of parents said they'd "seriously considered getting rid of [their TV] altogether" because it airs too much sex and bad language. But at the same time, for parents of the youngest viewers—ages 2 to 5—there are new reasons for optimism. Now that PBS, which invented the good-for-kids genre, has new competition from Nickelodeon and Disney, there are more quality choices for preschoolers than ever.

Inside those networks, a growing number of Ph.D.s are injecting the latest in child-development theory into new programs. In Disney's "Stanley," meet a freckle-faced kid who's fascinated with animals; in one episode, he and his pals explore the life and habitat of a platypus. Nickelodeon now airs 4.5 hours of quality preschool shows daily (in addition to learning-free fare like "SpongeBob" for older kids). Shows like "Dora" and "Blue's Clues" goad kids into interacting with the television set; studies show this improves problem-solving skills. Even the granddaddy of this genre, "Sesame Street," has undergone a makeover to better serve today's precocious viewers. The newcomers provide stiff competition to Mister Rogers, whose show stopped production in 2000 (it still airs on PBS). But he welcomes his new TV neighbors. "I'm just glad that more producers—and purveyors of television—have signed the pledge to protect child-hood," says Fred Rogers, who now writes parenting books.

That's the good news. The bad news is that working these shows into kids' lives in a healthy way remains a challenge. Much of what kids watch remains banal or harmful. Many kids watch too much. There are also troubling socioeconomic factors at work. In lower-income homes, for instance, kids watch more and are more likely to have TV in their bedrooms, a practice pediatricians discourage. But even as some families choose to go TV-free, more parents are recognizing that television can be beneficial. In the Public Agenda survey, 93 percent of parents agree that "TV is fine for kids as long as he or she is watching the right shows and watching in moderation."

When it comes to the right shows, "Sesame Street" remains the gold standard. Last week, as the crew taped an episode for its 34th season, the set looked comfortingly familiar: while Telly and Baby Bear worked on a skit near Hooper's Store, Snuffleupagus hung from the rafters, sleeping under a sheet. The show's longevity is a testament to the research-driven process founder Joan Ganz Cooney invented in the late 1960s. Then, as now, each season begins with Ph.D.s working alongside writers to set goals and review scripts. Any time there's a question—will kids understand Slimey the Worm's mission to the moon?—they head to day-care centers to test the material.

When "Sesame" began reinventing kids' TV in the early '70s, Daniel Anderson was a newly minted professor of psychology at the University of Massachusetts, Amherst. Like most child-development pros at that time, he assumed TV was bad for kids. Then one day Anderson taught his class that young children have very short attention spans. One student challenged him: "So why do kids sit still for an hour to watch 'Sesame Street'?" "I genuinely didn't know the answer," Anderson recalls. So he went to a lab and placed kids in front of TVs to find it.

What he found surprised him. Like most researchers, he assumed that fast-moving images and sounds mesmerized young viewers. But videotapes of kids' viewing showed that their attention wandered most during transitions between segments and when dialogue or plotlines became too complex. He hypothesized that even young children watch TV for the same reason adults do: to enjoy good stories. To test that theory, he sliced up "Sesame Street" skits so the plot no longer made sense. Even 2-year-olds quickly realized the story was amiss and stopped watching. Some knocked on the TV screen. Others called out: "Mommy, can you fix this?" Over years of research, Anderson reached a startling conclusion: "Television viewing is a much more intellectual activity for kids than anybody had previously supposed."

This research might have stayed hidden in psych journals if it hadn't been for the work of two equally powerful forces: the U.S. Congress and a purple dinosaur named Barney. In 1990 Congress passed the Children's Television Act, increasing demand for quality kids' shows. Then "Barney & Friends" was launched as a PBS series in 1992. Kids went wild, and merchandise flew off shelves. Until then, Nickelodeon and Disney had been content to leave preschool shows to the do-gooders at PBS. Now they saw gold. "The success of 'Barney' just changed everybody's feeling—it became 'OK, we should be able to do that, too'," says Marjorie Kalins, a former "Sesame" executive.

It was a profitable move. By 2001 Nick and Disney's TV businesses had generated a combined $1.68 billion in revenue, according to Paul Kagan Associates. Everyone admits that licensing money influences programming decisions. (Ironically, merchandisers at Nickelodeon lobbied against "Dora" because they believed that another show would generate more sales.) Ads and toys can detract from many parents' enthusiasm for the shows; no matter how much your kid may learn from "Sagwa" or "Rolie Polie Olie," the characters are hard to love when you can't get through Wal-Mart without a giant case of "I-WANT-itis."

Until there's a way to make shows free, that overcommercialization will continue. But for parents, there's some comfort from knowing that more TV producers are applying the latest research to make their shows better. This happened partly because researchers of Anderson's generation helped grow a new crop of Ph.D.s, who began graduating into jobs at "Sesame" and Nickelodeon. And like seeds from a dande-

Kirkman and Scott. © by Baby Blues Partnership. Reproduced by permission of King Features Syndicate.

lion blown at by a child, folks who'd trained at "Sesame" began taking root inside other networks. Anne Sweeney, who'd studied at Harvard with "Sesame" cofounder Gerald Lesser, interned with television activist Peggy Charren and spent 12 years at Nickelodeon, took over the Disney Channel in 1996. She hired a team (led by ex-Nick programmer Rich Ross) to design preschool shows. By 1999 Disney had a full block of little-kid programming it branded Playhouse Disney. Today it uses a 28-page "Whole Child Curriculum" detailing what shows should teach.

To see how research can drive these new-generation shows, come along, neighbor, as we visit a day-care center on Manhattan's Upper West Side. Dr. Christine Ricci sits in a child-size chair, holding a script and tapping a red pen against her lip. Ricci, who holds a psychology Ph.D. from UMass, is research director for "Dora the Explorer," which airs on Nick Jr., Nickelodeon's preschool block. In each episode Dora, an animated Latina girl, goes on a journey with a monkey named Boots. Using a map to guide them (which helps kids' spatial skills), they visit three locations ("Waterfall, mountain, forest!" kids yell) and solve problems. As in "Blue's Clues," Nick Jr.'s groundbreaking hit in which a dog named Blue and the host Joe help kids solve puzzles, "Dora" encourages kids to yell back at the screen (often in Spanish) or do physical movements (like rowing a boat).

Today Ricci shows 4-year-olds a crudely animated "Dora" episode slated for next season. As they watch, Ricci's team charts, moment by moment, whether the kids are paying attention and interacting with the screen. At first the kids sit transfixed, but during a pivotal scene (in which Swiper the fox, Dora's nemesis, throws a boot down a hole) their attention wanders. One child picks up a Magic Marker, and suddenly every child is seeking out toys. All the while the researchers scribble furiously. When the episode ends, an adult asks the children questions: "What color button on the fix-it machine matched the tire?" Their recall is astonishing. "Sesame Street" has done this kind of testing off and on since the '70s. Ricci's team, however, is relentless, testing and revising every "Dora" episode repeatedly.

The following afternoon, Ricci, "Dora" creator Chris Gifford and their team study a bar graph showing how kids interacted with the episode minute by minute. To boost the numbers, sometimes they suggest better animation. Sometimes they call for a better "money shot": a big close-up of

Dora. Fixing one segment—"Only 15 out of 26 kids were still watching," Ricci informs them gravely—requires more drastic measures. Gifford stands up, motioning like a cheerleader, to suggest livelier movements to get kids moving along with Dora during a song. "So often when you work on a TV show for kids, you forget about your audience," Gifford says. "We've set up a system where we can't ignore them." Similar work goes on at "Blue's Clues." Says Nick Jr. chief Brown Johnson: "It's science meets story."

For a parent, it's natural to get excited when kids shout back at the TV during "Dora" or dance to "The Wiggles," a music-and-dance show that airs on Disney. That leads some parents to look at their TVs the way a previous generation looked to Dr. Spock. Colleen Breitbord of Framingham, Mass., sees these programs as so vital to the development of her children, 7 and 2, that she installed a TV in the kitchen so they can watch "Arthur" and "Clifford" while they eat. "They learn so much," Breitbord says. "I think children who don't have the opportunity to watch some of this excellent programming miss out." In Ansonia, Conn., Patti Sarandrea uses Playhouse Disney, Nick Jr. and PBS "to reinforce what I teach the kids: colors, shapes, counting." At 3½, her daughter can count to 25. Thanks to "Dora," her 18-month-old says "Hola."

As kids that young start tuning in, even "Sesame" is rethinking its approach. The show was originally designed for kids 3 to 5, but by the mid-1990s, many viewers were 2 or younger. The tykes seemed to tire of 60 minutes of fast-paced Muppet skits (the pacing was originally modeled after "Laugh-In" and TV commercials). So in 1999 "Sesame" introduced "Elmo's World," a 15-minute segment that ended every show. Even after that change, "Sesame" VP Lewis Bernstein noticed how today's little kids would sit still to watch 90-minute videotaped movies. So last February "Sesame" unveiled more longer segments. In "Journey to Ernie," Big Bird and Ernie play hide-and-seek against an animated background. Today ratings are up. The cast likes the new format, too. Before, stories were constantly cut short. "It was a little discombobulating," says Kevin Clash, the muscular, deep-voiced Muppet captain who brings Elmo to life. Now Elmo l-o-o-o-ves the longer stories.

So just how much good do these shows do? On a recent afternoon five undergrads sit around a table in the Yale University psychology department, playing a bizarre variation of bingo to try to find out. Together they watch three episodes of "Barney & Friends," each filling in hash marks on six sheets of paper. After each screening, they tally how many "teaching elements" they've counted. "I've got 9 vocabulary, 6 numbers . . . 11 sharing," says one student. Afterward Yale researcher Dorothy Singer will crunch the data and compare them with past seasons'. Her work has shown that the higher an episode's score, the more accurately children will be able to recount the plot and use the vocabulary words.

PBS does more of this postproduction "summative" research than other networks. Study after study shows "Sesame" viewers are better prepared for school. "Dragon Tales," a "Sesame"-produced animated show, helps kids become more goal-oriented, and "Between the Lions," a puppet show produced by Boston's WGBH, helps kids' reading. Nick research offers proof of the effectiveness of "Dora" and "Blue's Clues." Disney doesn't do summative research; Disney execs say for now they'd rather devote resources to creating more shows for new viewers. Competitors suggest another reason: Disney's shows may not measure up. "It's scary to test," says "Sesame" research chief Rosemarie Truglio. "Maybe that's a piece of it—they're afraid."

Network-funded research won't change the minds of folks who say kids are better off with no television at all. That view gained strength in 1999, when the American Academy of Pediatrics began discouraging any television for kids under 2. But when you parse the pro- and anti-TV rhetoric, the two sides don't sound as far apart as you'd suspect. The pro-TV crowd, for instance, quickly concedes that violent TV is damaging to kids, and that too many kids watch too many lousy shows. The anti-TV crowd objects mostly to TV's widespread overuse. Like Häagen-Dazs, TV seems to defy attempts at moderation, they suggest, so it's safer to abstain entirely. They believe overviewing especially affects children because of what Marie Winn, author of *The Plug-In Drug*, calls the "displacement factor." That's when kids watch so much TV that they don't engage in enough brain-enhancing free play as toddlers or read enough during elementary school. Although pro-TV researchers say there are no data to support those fears, they agree it could be true. In fact, Anderson is currently conducting an experiment to measure whether having adult shows (like "Jeopardy!") playing in the background interferes with children's play. Bad news, soap-opera fans: the early data suggest it might.

Even shows the academics applaud could be better. In his UMass office, Anderson pops in a videotape of "Dora." It's one of the handful of shows that he advised during their conception. In this episode, Dora and Boots paddle a canoe down a river, around some rocks, toward a waterfall. Toward a waterfall? "If I'd read this script I'd have completely blocked this," he says, because it models unsafe behavior. Anderson has his arms crossed, his eyebrows scrunched; occasionally he talks to the screen, like an NFL fan disputing a bad call. "Oh, God, another dangerous thing," he says as Dora and Boots canoe under downed tree limbs. He still likes "Dora," but not this episode. "The education is a little thinner than I would wish, and it's a little dubious sending them on such a dumb journey." Then he watches "Bear" and "Blue's Clues," still nitpicking but happier.

Even as the kids' TV environment improves, shortcomings remain. Only PBS airs educational shows for older elementary kids (examples: "Zoom" and "Cyberchase"). In focus groups, says Nickelodeon president Herb Scannell, older kids say they get enough learning in school; what commercial broadcaster is going to argue with the audience? Producers have other worries. Mitchell Kriegman, creator of "Bear in the Big Blue House," says parents could grow too enamored of obviously educational, A-B-C/1-2-3-type shows. One of the most successful episodes of "Bear" involves potty training. "The [network's] reaction was 'Oh, my God, you can't say poop and pee on TV'," Kriegman says. "Bear" did, and families loved it. Tighter curricula could dampen that creativity.

But those are worries for the future. For now, it's worth celebrating the improvements—however incremental—in shows for TV's youngest audience. Not everyone will want to raise a glass: like alcohol or guns, TV will be used sensibly in some homes and wreak havoc in others. Debating its net societal value will remain a never-ending pursuit. In the meantime parents live through these trade-offs daily. A recent issue of *Parenting* magazine offered the following question to help assess parenting skills: "I let my child watch TV only when . . . A) There's an educational show on public television, B) I have time to narrate the action for him . . . or C) I want to take a shower." The scoring code rates the answers: "A) Liar, B) Big fat liar, and C) You may not be perfect, but at least you're honest." As kids' TV raises the bar, parents who choose a different answer—D) All of the above—have a little less reason to feel guilty.

*"People who eat fast food twice a week and
spend at least 2½ hours a day watching
television have* triple *the risk of . . .
obesity."*

Television Is Responsible for
the Obesity Epidemic

Ron Kaufman

Journalist and teacher Ron Kaufman created the Kill Your
Television Web site to convince people to reduce the time
they spend watching television, which he believes is harmful.
He alleges in the following viewpoint that TV viewing is a
main contributor to the rise of obesity in the United States.
Children who spend a lot of time in front of the television
are likely to snack on junk food and generally do not engage
in enough exercise, which can lead to obesity, Kaufman
maintains. Being grossly overweight is problematic, he
points out, because it is associated with a plethora of alarming health conditions, including heart disease and diabetes.
According to experts cited by Kaufman, children should
watch very little television and should get involved in other
activities in order to prevent obesity.

As you read, consider the following questions:
1. What percent of people with diabetes are overweight,
   according to the CDC?
2. According to Kaufman, what are "tweens" and what does
   the VERB campaign encourage them to do?
3. In the author's contention, how many commercials is the
   average American exposed to each year?

"In 1999, an estimated 61 percent of U.S. adults were over-weight, along with 13 percent of children and adolescents. Only 3 percent of all Americans meet at least four of the five federal Food Guide Pyramid recommendations for the intake of grains, fruits, vegetables, dairy products, and meats. And less than one-third of Americans meet the federal recommendations to engage in at least 30 minutes of moderate physical activity at least five days a week, while 40 percent of adults engage in no leisure-time physical activity at all."

—from "The Surgeon General's Call to Action to Prevent and Decrease Overweight and Obesity," December 2001.

A mericans are getting fatter. The modern lifestyle of computer screens, video games and television is resulting in Americans not exercising and eating poorly. Though computers and video games certainly have an effect on diet and lack of exercise, no medium is more widespread throughout the United States than television. The United States is home to 281 million people, 219 million television sets, more than 1,500 individual TV broadcast stations, and about 9,000 different cable systems. Americans watch a lot of TV, eat a lot of junk food, and don't exercise enough.

The Problem of Obesity in America

The number of children, teenagers and adults that are overweight and obese is quite alarming. The US government's Health and Human Services Department (HHS) reports that nearly 61 percent of US adults and 13 percent of children and adolescents are overweight. The number of overweight adolescents has tripled since 1980. Of the 61 percent of overweight adults, nearly half are characterized as obese. And the numbers are rising. Health officials estimate that [by 2008], four out of 10 adults will be obese.

Overweight means that someone possesses an excess of body fat (measured by a Body Mass Index). The common statistic is that women should have 20 percent body fat, while men should have 15 percent. Women with more than 30 percent fat and men with more than 25 percent fat are considered obese.

The HHS Centers for Disease Control and Prevention (CDC) estimates that 300,000 deaths a year are caused by obesity. Other health concerns due to poor weight control are increase in heart disease, high blood pressure, diabetes type 2 (the CDC says more than 80 percent of people with diabetes are overweight), increased risk of cancer, breathing problems, arthritis, reproductive complications, gall bladder disease, and other problems. Weight problems are also associated with depression, limited mobility and decreased physical endurance.

TV Viewing Is a Preventable Cause of Obesity

Watching TV causes weight gain in children. The [American] Academy [of Pediatrics] said in 1999, "Increased television use is documented to be a significant factor leading to obesity. . . ."

This is important for two reasons. First, excess weight is a significant, and worsening, problem among American children. Roughly 25% of U.S. children are overweight or obese. Secondly, children who are overweight turn into adults who tend to be overweight as well, and the *Journal of the American Medical Association* said in 1999 that *excessive weight gain among American adults is an "epidemic"* and a major cause of disease and death. . . .

Fast foods and snack foods, and the barrage of advertisements that induce us to eat them, are having an effect on many of us. And a sedentary lifestyle is taking its toll, too. Just recently a study published in the *Journal of the American Medical Association* showed that children lost weight, and lost inches around the midriff, if they simply watched less TV. . . .

Excess weight is a major public health problem, and television viewing is an important—and preventable—contributing factor.

Dr. Jon, "Your TV Does Much More than Show Pictures," Alternative Medicine Research Foundation. www.cat007.com/tv.htm.

In July 2002, the CDC launched a campaign called "VERB: It's What You Do!" to try and increase awareness about these problems in children. The campaign focuses on increasing physical activity and improving diet. Overweight and obese children will often become overweight adults. The VERB press release states it is "a national, multicultural media campaign intended to promote physical activity and community involvement and displace unhealthy, risky behaviors among 9- to 13-year-olds," an age group known in marketing terms as "tweens." The campaign encourages tweens to find a verb (such as run, paint, sing, dance, jump, skate, etc.)

or several verbs that fit their personality and interests. The campaign then encourages tweens to use "their verb" as a launching pad to better health and make regular physical activity and community involvement a lifetime pursuit."

Children Watch Too Much TV

The CDC notes that "one-fourth of children in America spend four hours or more *watching television* daily and only 27 percent of students in grades 9 through 12 engage in moderate physical activity at least 30 minutes a day on five or more days of the week."

According to the CDC, lifestyle behaviors is one of the major factors contributing to obesity in children and adults. Genetics does play a role; however, many health risks have been proved to significantly diminish when physical activity increases and diet improves. One major suggestion by health officials is a reduction in "screen time." The VERB campaign promotes a decrease in time spent in a sedentary TV-watching position and replace it with positive physical and prosocial activities. [The *VERB Fact Sheet* reads:]

"The average tween spends four and a half hours each day in front of a screen. This includes watching television, videotapes or DVDs, playing video games, using a computer or browsing the Internet. *Television is the medium with which children spend the most time*—two and a half hours each day.

• 26 percent of U.S. children watch four or more hours of television per day.

• 67 percent of U.S. children watch two or more hours per day.

• Almost half (48 percent) of all families with tweens have all four of the latest media staples: TV, VCR, video game equipment and a computer.

• The bedroom of the 21st century child is a multimedia environment. *Of children 9–13 years old, more than half (57 percent) have a TV in the bedroom;* 39 percent have video game equipment; 30 percent have a VCR; 20 percent a computer and 11 percent Internet access."

Television's Negative Influence

The American Academy of Pediatrics (AAP) issued a position paper in February 2001 which noted that its research has shown that "children and adolescents are particularly vulnerable to the messages conveyed through television, which influence their perceptions and behaviors. Many younger children cannot discriminate between what they see and what is real. Research has shown primary negative health effects on violence and aggressive behavior; sexuality; academic performance; body concept and self-image; nutrition, dieting, and obesity; and substance use and abuse patterns."

The AAP report went on to present some moderate guidelines that pediatricians should recommend to parents:

1. Limit children's total media time (with entertainment media) to no more than 1 to 2 hours of quality programming per day.
2. Remove television sets from children's bedrooms.
3. Discourage television viewing for children younger than 2 years, and encourage more interactive activities that will promote proper brain development, such as talking, playing, singing, and reading together.
4. Monitor the shows children and adolescents are viewing. Most programs should be informational, educational, and nonviolent.
5. View television programs along with children, and discuss the content. Two recent surveys involving a total of nearly 1500 parents found that less than half of parents reported always watching television with their children.
6. Use controversial programming as a stepping-off point to initiate discussions about family values, violence, sex and sexuality, and drugs.
7. Use the videocassette recorder wisely to show or record high-quality, educational programming for children.
8. Support efforts to establish comprehensive media-education programs in schools.
9. Encourage alternative entertainment for children, including reading, athletics, hobbies, and creative play.

Healthy Eating

Television does not promote a healthy lifestyle. Junk food advertising can be viewed with regularity on TV. The whole "process" of watching television is not an active one. And most likely, the diet accompanying TV-watching is high in sugar, fat and calories. Television is Doritos, Cheetos and Lucky Charms. Television is Coors, Budweiser and Miller Genuine Draft. Television is sitting in a sofa and not moving. And there's nothing jovial about McDonald's "Happy Meals."

Advertising Age reports that $46 billion was spent on TV advertising in 2001. Obviously, television advertising is big money. In 2001, Anheuser-Busch spent $285 million to promote Bud Light, Michelob and others on TV—Coca-Cola spent $357 million—General Mills spent $510 million to talk up the Pillsbury Doughboy and Bugles corn chips—McDonald's spent $590 million—and PepsiCo spent $570 million marketing Frito-Lay and Pepsi-Cola on TV. Believe it or not, all these numbers are actually down from the previous year. The result of all this huge expenditure is that regular-viewing American television audiences are exposed to between 10,000 and 20,000 commercials a year. Corporations spend millions on TV ads for a reason: they work.

Research suggests that food choices are, in part, affected by TV advertising and that most TV advertising is for food with questionable nutritional value. . . .

A study presented to the American Heart Association on March 9, 2003, shows a strong link between obesity, fast food, and television watching. Researcher Mark Pereira, of Boston's Children's Hospital, presented data that showed a 50 percent greater risk of obesity for people who eat fast food twice or more a week. This same group had double the risk of abnormal glucose control and an inability to break down sugar. Pereira also noted that people who eat fast food twice a week and spend at least 2½ hours a day watching television have *triple* the risk of both obesity and abnormal glucose control when compared to those who eat out once or less and watch no more than an hour and a half of TV.

"It's clearly the composition of fast-food meals that we feel plays a role, with a lot of saturated fat and low-quality carbohydrates, white bread and lots of soda," said Pereira. "It's a dietary pattern that is opposite of what's recommended for health."

Eating healthy is easy. Cut down on junk food snacking while sitting in front of the TV (or eliminate the TV entirely). . . .

Regular Exercise Is Much More Productive than Watching TV

Along with healthy eating is regular exercise. Without exercise, weight cannot be lost and real health gains are not achieved. The President's Council on Physical Fitness issued a brochure that shows calories used per hour in a variety of activities (for an 150 pound (68 kg) person): light housework burns off 246 calories per hour; swimming burns 288; walking burns 198; scrubbing floors burns 440; jogging burns 654; bicycling burns 612; weight training burns off 756; *and sitting quietly watching TV burns off 84.* Considering that six restaurant-style corn chips have about 150 calories (plus 8 grams of fat) and four creme-filled cookies have around 220 calories (or more), it is obvious that watching TV will not help anyone lose weight.

Aerobic exercise will burn calories, strengthen the heart and muscles and condition the lungs. The word "aerobic" is Greek and means "with oxygen." The more oxygen that is used, the more the body has to work to create energy. The body gets energy from fat cells and burning those cells is what produces weight loss. According to the CDC and President's Council, an average person should engage in at least 20–40 minutes of physical aerobic exercise at least three times a week. This is actually a lot less time than most people spend watching TV.

"TV, like junk food or lack of exercise, does not cause obesity. Obesity is caused by far too much food, eaten unconsciously throughout the day."

Television Is Not to Blame for the Obesity Epidemic

Frank Furedi

Frank Furedi, author of *Paranoid Parenting*, is a professor of sociology at the University of Kent. In the viewpoint that follows, he discusses the mounting problem of childhood obesity and cautions that parents should not fault television for the increasing number of overweight youths. Although he acknowledges that while people watch TV they tend to eat more and to expend less energy, he proposes that poor eating habits, not TV itself, is responsible for obesity. He identifies constant snacking, especially in front of the TV, as the major culprit. In order to combat obesity, Furedi reasons, families should establish consistent eating patterns by having regularly scheduled meals.

As you read, consider the following questions:
1. What does the author say about the quality of food consumed by children over the past century?
2. Name three reasons that scheduled meals are important, according to Furedi.
3. In the author's opinion, when does snacking become a problem?

Frank Furedi, "The Food Wars: Fed Up with Too Many Snacks?" Voices (Madrina.com). Reproduced by permission of the author.

S tatistics are useful for alerting us to a new pattern of childhood life, [yet] this information does not necessarily tell us what the root of the problem is, or what, if anything, we can do about it. Parents are often subject to conflicting and unhelpful advice.

Health promotion and food campaigners generally blame poor diet for the rise in obesity, and junk food is a ready-made target. Such campaigns, though well-meaning, say more about adult food obsessions than about the problem facing children. For while there are many good arguments for children eating healthy food, reducing childhood obesity is not one of them. There is little evidence to suggest that the quality of food consumed by children has deteriorated over the past century. Despite the scare stories, generally their diet has improved. Yet the number of obese children is rising.

There has also been a blame on lack of exercise. Today, fewer children walk or cycle to school. Parental anxieties about the risks facing their offspring outdoors are partly to blame and, as schools reduce the time that pupils have for play and sports, the physical life of children diminishes. It is not surprising that the contraction of children's physical activity coincides with the expansion of non-physical play: a large portion of their free time is now devoted to TV and computer games.

Food Wars

By all means, let us do whatever we can to improve the physical life of children. However, focusing on this issue may well distract attention from the fact that, ultimately, obesity is bound up with the way we eat. It is not simply a problem but a symptom of the difficulty that parents face in managing children's eating habits. As every parent knows, children are very good at using food as a weapon. Refusing to eat certain types of food, or even any food, demanding a treat in the supermarket, declining to sit while eating, or consuming food in front of the TV, are just some tactics used by children in the food war. These tactics are used to test boundaries and to demand attention and, inadvertently, parental anxiety about children's eating habits only encourages this.

Soon, the so-called picky eater or the constant snacker

To examine the relationships between hours of television viewing and adiposity and physical activity among female adolescents, a cohort study with follow-up assessments 7, 14, and 24 months after baseline was conducted. All sixth- and seventh-grade girls attending four northern California middle schools were eligible to participate. . . . The baseline sample had a mean age of 12.4 years and was 43% white, 22% Asian, 21% Latino, 6% Pacific Islander, 4% black, 2% American Indian, and 2% other. Hours of after-school television viewing, level of physical activity, and stage of sexual maturation were assessed with self-report instruments. Height, weight, and triceps skinfold thickness were measured. . . . [To determine whether each girl was obese,] body mass index (ratio of weight [in kilograms] to height [in meters] squared) and triceps skinfold thickness were adjusted by level of sexual maturity for the analyses. Baseline hours of after-school television viewing was not significantly associated with either baseline or longitudinal change in body mass index or triceps skinfold thickness. Baseline hours of after-school television viewing was weakly negatively associated with level of physical activity in cross-sectional analyses but not significantly associated with change in level of physical activity over time. All results were essentially unchanged when adjusted for age, race, parent education, and parent fatness. Among adolescent girls, television viewing time appears to have only weak, if any, meaningful associations with adiposity, physical activity, or change in either over time.

Thomas N. Robinson et al., *Pediatrics*, February 1993.

gains the upper hand, and the main casualty of this struggle is the regular family meal. Most children still have regular meals but they often regard eating as an activity that, although it begins at the meal table, invariably continues on a tray in another room. And with this dissociation of eating from the meal comes the institutionalisation of snacking. A meal has a definite beginning and an end. After a meal, both parent and child know what and how much has been eaten. The meal provides parents with an opportunity to teach children appropriate eating behaviour, and helps children to manage their appetites. This is a time when children can adopt a regular pattern of eating.

Snacking and TV Viewing

Snacking always contains the potential for creating a chaotic eating pattern. It makes it difficult for parents to monitor just how much their children are eating.

Constant snacking also distracts children from getting in touch with their appetites. It encourages an attitude in which food is consumed as a form of distraction rather than as a way of dealing with hunger. Of course, there is nothing wrong with the occasional snack. It is when the snack competes with or becomes an alternative to the meal that there is an issue. Snacking turns eating into an activity that is an adjunct of doing something else. This problem is particularly striking in relation to watching TV.

Research indicates that childhood obesity is strongly associated with TV. A recent report, published in the *American Journal of Paediatrics*, concluded that "a TV in the child's bedroom is the strongest marker of increased risk of being overweight". The study confirms previous research which has shown that obesity is linked clearly to the hours a child spends watching television. This is because watching TV not only reduces energy expenditure, it also increases food intake. And food advertisements, which tend to promote snacks, have an important effect on children's eating habits, helping to perpetuate the cycle of unconscious eating, as [one] study published in the *Journal of the American Dietetic Association* claimed. . . . Through such advertising, children are effectively encouraged to regard snacking as a routine part of viewing.

In another study, Thomas Robinson, a professor of paediatrics at Stanford University School of Medicine, says that the most effective way of preventing obesity is to reduce children's TV viewing because this will, in turn, reduce their calorie intake. So yes, increased exercise is important, but the real issue is the way children eat.

Television Is Not to Blame

But it is important not to blame TV itself for the difficulty that parents face in holding the line at the dinner table. TV, like junk food or lack of exercise, does not cause obesity.

97

Obesity is caused by far too much food, eaten unconsciously throughout the day.

The meal provides a unique opportunity to structure youngsters' eating habits and to manage the chaotic world of eating. Getting children to take their meals seriously is the one battle worth fighting.

"*Reality TV allows audiences to laugh, cry, and live vicariously through . . . ordinary people who . . . experience things that . . . most individuals only dream about.*"

Reality TV Is Inspiring

Cynthia M. Frisby

In the viewpoint that follows, Cynthia M. Frisby, coeditor of *Journalism Across Cultures*, hails reality TV programs for benefiting society. Frisby argues that reality shows improve viewers' moods and their self-esteem. Specifically, she claims that viewers who follow the successes or hardships of reality show participants become more grateful about their own lives, inspired to accomplish their goals, and better able to cope with their problems.

As you read, consider the following questions:

1. Name the six gratifications of media use, as cited by Frisby.
2. How does the author define upward and downward comparisons?
3. In Frisby's study, who was categorized as "regular" viewers of reality TV?

Cynthia M. Frisby, "Getting Real with Reality TV," *USA Today*, vol. 133, September 2004, p. 50. Copyright © 2004 by the Society for the Advancement of Education. Reproduced by permission.

Every year, television networks vie to create cutting edge programming. New shows promise more drama, suspense, and laughter while pushing the envelope of what is morally and socially acceptable, funny, thrilling, and, of course, entertaining. Fitting all these criteria—at least according to the soaring ratings—is reality based television.

Reality TV is a genre of programming in which the everyday routines of "real life" people (as opposed to fictional characters played by actors) are followed closely by the cameras. Viewers cannot seem to help but become involved in the captivating plotlines and day-to-day drama depicted daily on their screens. Apparently, people simply take pleasure in watching other people's lives while those under scrutiny enjoy being on television enough to go on for free.

There are three major categories within the reality genre: game shows (e.g., "Survivor"), dating shows (e.g., "The Bachelor"), and talent shows (e.g., "American Idol"). While reality programming breeds fiercely during the regular season, in summer there is an even greater glut since such programs are cheap to produce and, if they fail to draw ratings, they quickly can be flushed away and replaced with something else.

Reality TV Shows Highlight Real-Life Concerns

It is becoming increasingly difficult to avoid contact with reality TV these days. In offices, hair salons, health clubs, restaurants, and bars, the general public is discussing what happened on television the night before—and it is not the world news they are dissecting. Rather, the hot topic may be what happened on "The Apprentice." Then again, it might be a "did-you-see" conversation concerning "The Bachelor" or "For Love or Money."

Shows such as "The Apprentice," "Survivor," "Fear Factor," "The Amazing Race," "American Idol," "American Girl," "Big Brother," "Extreme Makeover," "Temptation Island," "Cheaters," "The Simple Life," "Queer Eye for the Straight Guy," "The Bachelor," and "The Bachelorette" have reached out and grabbed today's American television viewer. Dining the 2003–04 season, 10 reality shows ranked among the top 25 prime-time programs in the audience-composition index for adults 18–49 with incomes of $75,000 or more.

Nielsen ratings indicate that more than 18,000,000 viewers have been captivated by television programs that take ordinary people and place them in situations that have them competing in ongoing contests while being filmed 24 hours a day. What is it about these shows that attracts millions of loyal viewers week after week? Is it blatant voyeurism, or can their success be explained as a harmless desire for entertainment?

From "Survivor" to "Elimidate" to "Average Joe" to "Joe Millionaire," it seems that reality TV succeeds because it plays off of real-life concerns—looking for love, competing to win a job or big prize, or becoming a millionaire—situations (or dreams) that most people can relate to. However, as these shows become more pervasive, their grip on "reality" seems to be growing more tenuous.

"It's refreshing to see everyday people getting some of the spotlight, rather than just seeing movie stars all the time," maintains CBS News associate Presley Weir. According to CBS, the same element of being human that encourages people to gossip about the lives of their friends, family, and even total strangers is what fosters an audience for reality television. Much like a car crash on the side of the freeway, glimpses into the interior workings of other human beings is often shocking, yet impossible to turn away from. It was this theory that produced MTV's "The Real World," often referred to as "the forerunner of reality television shows." Seven strangers are selected to live together, and viewers watch to find out what happens when individuals with different backgrounds and points of view are left in close quarters.

Media Gratification and Social Comparison Theory

Researchers frequently refer to at least six gratifications of media use: information (also known as surveillance or knowledge), escape, passing time, entertainment, social viewing/status enhancement, and relaxation. Although the names or labels for these gratifications may change, various studies confirm that they hold up in and across all situations. So what type of gratifications do viewers receive from reality TV?

Social comparison theory may help to explain and uncover an important motive—which many people may be unable, or unwilling, to express openly—for watching reality television. Psychologists define social comparison as "the process of thinking about information about one or more people in relation to the self." Social comparison theory postulates that individuals have a drive or need to compare their abilities and opinions to others. In 1954, Leon Festinger, who coined the theory and pioneered research in this area, believed that people who are uncertain about their abilities and opinions will evaluate themselves by making comparisons with similar others.

Actually, individuals compare themselves with others for a variety of reasons, including to: determine relative standing on an issue or related ability; emulate behaviors; determine norms; lift spirits or feel better about life and personal situations; and evaluate emotions, personality, and self-worth.

Those made with others who are superior to or better off than oneself are referred to as upward comparisons. Individuals engaging in upward comparison may learn from others, be inspired by their examples, and become highly motivated to achieve similar goals. Upward comparisons, research suggests, are invoked when a person is motivated to change or overcome difficulties. Self-improvement is the main effect of an upward comparison because the targets serve as role models, teaching and motivating individuals to achieve or overcome similar problems.

On the other hand, when a social comparison involves a target who is inferior, incompetent, or less fortunate, it is referred to as a downward comparison. Its basic principle is that people feel better about their own situation and enhance their subjective well-being when they make comparisons with others who are worse off. Supposedly, downward comparisons help individuals cope with personal problems by allowing them to see themselves and their difficulties in a more positive light by realizing there are others who face more difficult circumstances.

Social Comparisons May Be Unconscious

A social comparison does not mean that the individual has to give careful, elaborate, conscious thought about the comparison but implies that there has to be, to some degree, an attempt to identify or look for similarities or differences between the other and the self on some particular dimension. There are theorists who might argue that, for a comparison to be considered a comparison, the individual must be aware of the comparison and come into direct contact with the other person. However, psychologists have discovered that social comparisons do not require conscious or direct personal contact because fictional characters illustrated in the media can represent meaningful standards of comparison.

Reality TV Depicts Personal Relationships in a Way That Scripted Shows Can't

Reality TV is . . . the best thing to happen to television in several years. It has given the networks water-cooler buzz again; it has reminded viewers jaded by sitcoms and dramas why TV can be exciting; and at its best, it is teaching TV a new way to tell involving human stories. . . .

[Scripted] series like *CSI* and *Law & Order* . . . have characters as detailed and individuated as checkers pieces. By the time *Survivor* ends, you know its players better than you know *Law & Order*'s Detective Briscoe after 11 years. Likewise, the WB's *High School Reunion*, which brings together classmates after 10 years, is really asking whether you're doomed to live out your high school role—"the jock," "the nerd" or whatnot—for life. Last fall [2002] two scripted shows, *That Was Then* and *Do Over*, asked the same question but with cardboard characters and silly premises involving time travel. They got canceled. *High School Reunion* got a second season.

James Poniewozik, *Time*, February 17, 2003.

Data on social comparisons and media use suggest that everyday encounters with media images may provide viewers with information that encourages them to engage in an automatic, spontaneous social comparison. This ultimately affects mood and other aspects of subjective well-being. People just might not be able to articulate consciously the comparison process or consciously register its effects (i.e., self-enhancement, self-improvement, etc.).

Reality TV allows audiences to laugh, cry, and live vicariously through so-called everyday, ordinary people who have opportunities to experience things that, until the moment they are broadcast, most individuals only dream about. Viewers may tune into these shows because they contain elements the audience would like to experience themselves; to laugh at the mistakes of others and/or celebrate successes; or to feel better about themselves because they are at least not as "bad as the people on television."

Exposure to tragic events or bad news invites social comparison among viewers. It is believed that reality audiences may be encouraged to compare and contrast their own situation with those of the reality show stars, and that this comparison process eventually could produce a form of self-satisfaction.

In real-life, everyday situations, it would be extremely difficult to avoid making some type of comparison. Frequently, people may compare themselves with others in their immediate environment or in the mass media in order to judge their own personal worth.

Evaluating How Viewers Respond to Reality TV

We contacted 110 people and asked them to complete a uses and gratifications survey on reality television with two goals in mind: to demonstrate that social comparisons may be elicited by certain television content, and to explore if viewers use reality television's content and images as a source for social comparison.

Of the respondents, 78.2% reported being regular viewers of reality television programs. A list of 37 reality shows was presented to the participants. They were asked to check those that they watch on a regular basis, and indicate on a scale of 1–5—number 1 signifying "liked a lot" and number five meaning "extreme dislike"—whether they liked or disliked each of the 37 programs. This paper-and-pencil test also asked respondents to identify the extent to which they considered themselves a "regular viewer of reality television." For purposes of conceptualization, a regular viewer was defined as "one who watches the show every week, and/or records episodes to avoid missing weekly broadcasts."

Data was obtained on other television viewing preferences by asking respondents to indicate how regularly they watch programs like news magazines, talk shows, reality programs, daytime serials, and other offerings and to identify the gratifications obtained from watching reality television.

To better understand the cognitive responses made when exposed to media content, a content analysis of the thoughts generated while watching reality TV was conducted. The researcher coded any and all thoughts that contained expressions of, or alluded to, social comparisons that participants "appeared to have" made spontaneously.

Participants were told that they later would see a segment of reality TV and encouraged to view that segment as if they were watching the program at home. While viewing the segment, participants were asked to record all their thoughts, and were given ample space to do so.

Data show that, of all the responses made concerning reality programming, most expressed some type of comparison between themselves and the reality show's stars. We conducted a content analyses of the thoughts and responses provided by the participants and found that, for the most part, men and women, as well as regular viewers and nonviewers, did not differ in terms of how they responded to people on reality shows.

We then compared mood ratings obtained prior to viewing the reality show with those from immediately following exposure to the program. Analysis clearly indicated that regular viewers and nonviewers alike experienced a significant mood enhancement after exposure to reality television.

Captivating Audiences

We know that reality television can captivate millions of viewers at any given time on any given day. Research has begun to document how people engage in automatic, spontaneous social comparisons when confronted by certain media images, particularly those of reality TV. We also know that one major effect of exposure to reality television is to feel better about one's own life circumstances, abilities, and talents.

Reality TV also serves as a much-needed distraction from the ongoing parade of tragic world events. It allows viewers an outlet by watching others overcome hardships, escape danger, live in a rainforest, land a dream job, learn to survive in Corporate America, and yes, even find love.

Whether the aim is money, love, becoming a rock star, creative expression, or just a chance to be seen on TV, the effect on audiences is the same. People like knowing that there are others who are going through the same life experiences that they are and often make the same mistakes. Despite the shifting desires of society and the fickleness of television audiences, the human need to compare and relate has provided a market for this genre.

So, while viewers realize they are not America's Next Top Model, may not have a chance at becoming the next American Idol, or even an All American Girl, they do enjoy the fact that, through a vicarious social comparison process, they can fall in love, win $1,000,000, or get the office snitch fired.

"Degradation, shaming and cruelty have become—appallingly—staples of popular entertainment."

Reality TV Is Dehumanizing

Melanie Phillips

Reality TV programs rely on cruelty and debauchery for viewer entertainment, charges Melanie Phillips in the following viewpoint. Reality show audiences regularly witness people being brutalized, which she claims is dangerously dehumanizing. Additionally, reality shows pervert social norms, Phillips argues, by advertising deviancy as acceptable and degradation as entertaining. She adds that reality shows foster contempt for contestants as well as for the lower social classes. Phillips is a journalist and author who has examined what she calls Great Britain's educational and moral crisis.

As you read, consider the following questions:

1. What are two goals of *Big Brother* producers, in the author's opinion?
2. According to Phillips, what is meant by "defining deviancy downwards"?
3. How does the author respond to the supposition that TV reflects the values of ordinary people?

There is a type of American satirical movie about the excesses of TV, which comically exaggerates reality by inventing fictional shows which are grotesque beyond belief in their quest for ratings. But in truth, nothing satire has created can match the real-life degradation of reality TV.

Contestants in the new Big Brother series include the following: a female bank clerk who was born a man, a lesbian who worked as a child prostitute, an air steward who says he was named 'Mr Best Buttocks South Lanarkshire' and says he has had 250 sexual partners, a gay man who claims to sleep only with straight men, and a student who calls himself 'the world's biggest bitch'.

Anything less like reality than this sad collection of troubled exhibitionists is hard to imagine. What is sickening is the brazen cynicism behind their recruitment. For there is now no limit to the stupid, gross or vile activities to which TV producers will encourage or subject people, so that viewers can jeer and sneer or get a sordid voyeuristic thrill.

Debauchery and Degradation on Reality TV

With every series, the behaviour encouraged on screen becomes ever more demeaning and sexually explicit. The aim is clear—to produce live sex close-up on TV. Contestants report the programme-makers appear to be obsessed with this unsavoury aim. The *Big Brother* house has only one bedroom with not enough beds, and transparent walls in the shower and lavatory.

As if this voyeurism isn't enough, the house has been made claustrophobic, apparently to encourage rows and violence. After live sex, can rape or even murder be far behind? For the problem with pushing back the boundaries of shockability like this is where this process leads.

But then, degradation, shaming and cruelty have become —appallingly—staples of popular entertainment. [Talk show hosts] Jerry Springer or Trisha [Goddard] do lifestyle trashing and humiliation; Anne Robinson [the *Weakest Link* host] or Ali G [who asks embarrassing questions during interviews] make people look very stupid through bullying or entrapment.

Shows such as *I'm a Celebrity . . . Get Me Out of Here* and *Wudja? Cudja?* invite contestants to perform revolting acts of self-abasement. *Footballers' Wives, Sin City, Temptation Island, Wife Swap, Take My Mother-in-Law*—the list goes on and on of programmes which pander to the very worst impulses of viewers towards either titillation or contempt for their fellow human beings.

Depravity Sells

There is apparently no area of life which can now escape the effects of televisual brutalisation. In *Hell's Kitchen*, the master chef Gordon Ramsay subjects his novices to tirades of foul-mouthed bullying over the bouillon. What next—gardening programmes featuring bestiality among the buddleia? House make-overs where home-owners drunkenly brawl and throw up over the furniture?

The terrible thing is that—although Ramsay's verbal onslaughts seem to have caused viewers to switch off—prurience on TV means profits. The quaint idea that TV has a duty to uphold standards of modesty, decency or self-restraint is laughed out of court as absurd and authoritarian prudery. Ratings are all that matter. So smart programme-makers with an eye on big careers do depravity TV. Degradation is where the modern TV reputation is made.

The brand leader in this field has long been Channel Four. But can the BBC be far behind? For in Michael Grade and Mark Thompson, Channel Four has now provided us with no less than the BBC's new Chairman [Grade] *and* Director-General [Thompson]. Mark Thompson's notable triumphs as chief executive of Channel Four included *Teen Big Brother*, featuring the gross spectacle of teenagers fumbling under a duvet [comforter], and, still to come, *The Sex Inspectors* in which couples will be filmed having sex, with their performance assessed by experts.

Of course, both men are making the right noises now about public service broadcasting. But what hope is there, when no less than [Great Britain's] Culture Secretary Tessa Jowell claimed . . . that reality TV was just another form of public service broadcasting because when the shows reached their climax they became a 'national talking point'? No doubt throwing Christians to the lions performed a similar function for the Romans, but even our most slavish devotees of popular culture would be hard put to describe that barbaric national spectacle as a public service.

Reality TV Is Heartless

A dinner party guest is ridiculed and told she's a fat monster; a father tells his family he is going to live on a tropical island and will never see them again; a young man tells his girlfriend he's gay—even though he's not. Welcome to a summer of reality TV. . . .

We want to see these [participants] squirm. We want to see them in tears; we want to see them angry; we want to see them humiliated. In short, we want to be cruel. . . .

There is a part of us which rejoices in seeing other people suffer. According to [cultural criminologist Mike] Presdee, this is partly a reaction to the constraints on our behaviour in public. If we can't be rude in public, at least we can laugh at them in private.

Nick Morrison, *This Is the North East*, June 9, 2003. www.thisisthenortheast. co.uk.

Why, though, is there this fixation with the lowest and most demeaning forms of human behaviour? It is all part of the wider phenomenon that has been termed 'defining deviancy downwards'. This turns what was once considered deviant or antisocial into acceptable behaviour.

Debauchery Is Becoming Mainstream

The idea that certain behaviour might deviate from society's norms is held to be oppressive, because such norms make people who contravene them feel bad about themselves—and feelings trump everything else. So the very concept of social norms has been junked, and deviancy defined not so much downwards as progressively out of existence.

This process becomes clear when you realise that what was once considered pornography is now mainstream entertainment on TV or in the cinema. So porn itself is being driven to ever greater extremes around paedophilia, anal sex or incest.

But as the goalposts shift our notion of what we should tolerate, our society is becoming ever more debauched. We have turned the men in dirty macs [raincoats] unisex, and sat them on the front-room sofa alongside grandma and the kids.

Yet however our cultural commissars redefine attitudes once thought deviant, they still remain brutalising, degrading and amoral. So why are we shocked to find that in the real world there is more violence, sadism, drunkenness, drug-taking and excess of every kind?

TV has become a theatre of cruelty and contempt. It supposedly champions the values of ordinary people. Indeed, the old . . . notion that television had a duty to elevate the tastes and attitudes of the masses is now dismissed as shockingly elitist and condescending. But in fact, so-called reality TV presents a savagely distorted view of the lower social classes that reflects only disgust and loathing for them.

The Dehumanisation of Voyeurs

It also embodies a devastating flight *from* reality. For people become voyeurs because their own lives are so hollow. They intrude into other people's intimacy because they cannot find intimacy themselves. They want to appropriate someone else's experience in the hope of filling a void.

Participating at a distance entails no emotional commitment. They face no consequences from such vicarious pseudo-experience. Far from reality, this is fantasy living and sets up a dangerous process of dehumanisation, particularly among vulnerable or suggestible characters who may translate these destructive lessons of emotional detachment into real life.

You can see the startling grip exercised by such fantasy worlds from the astonishing case of the boy who induced another teenager to murder him, through an elaborate deception involving multiple assumed personalities on the Internet. Both computers and TV serve up a form of virtual reality in which the key factor is emotional detachment.

With family breakdown fracturing the identities of the young on an epidemic scale, this society's grasp of reality is set to become ever more tenuous and all kinds of deviancy more commonplace.

Television does not merely reflect but helps shape the values of a culture. And by making the abnormal seem normal so that it becomes acceptable and even entertaining, unreality TV is doing the public a truly devastating disservice.

"Soul-mate hunting, it turns out, depends less upon the twists and turns of fate and much more upon a well-funded boyfriend search on national TV."

Reality TV Trivializes Marriage

Judith Halberstam

Judith Halberstam is an English professor and director of the Center for Feminist Research at the University of Southern California. In the following viewpoint she accuses reality TV of violating the sanctity of marriage. She denounces marriage shows on which a single man or woman narrows down a pool of contestants and proposes to the winner based solely on looks and sexual chemistry. Few of these couples actually marry, she points out. What's more, even on reality series that attempt to demonstrate that love is based on more than money and looks, contestants consistently choose money and looks above all else, maintains Halberstam.

As you read, consider the following questions:

1. What is Halberstam's objection to reality show bachelors and bachelorettes going on overnight dates with the final contestants?
2. In the author's opinion, why did *Boy Meets Boy* fail?
3. What would happen if interracial or lesbian trysts were depicted on marriage shows, in Halberstam's contention?

M arriage. Is it: (1) an intimate union recognized by the state, (2) the joining of man and woman in the eyes of God or (3) a competitive sport on network TV produced for the entertainment of millions? Anyone emerging recently from an isolation chamber . . . might be forgiven for believing that marriage has gone to the dogs (and the gays and the lesbians, for that matter) and become a game show. Indeed, young men and women are lining up to be chosen by complete strangers for lifetime commitments even as divorce rates hover at 50 percent. Why has marriage become primetime fodder for a public that craves escapist "reality" TV? Should we interpret these new marriage shows as evidence that the institution has completely crumbled or as a reinforcement of its ubiquity?

Reality marriage shows have angered conservatives who feel that the programs represent marriage as a kind of popularity contest. But one could easily argue that these shows take marriage for granted as a basic fact of life and revel in its endlessly fascinating details. Some gay and lesbian viewers have complained that these shows recentralize heterosexuality at a critical moment in the nation's marriage debates. And yet, the conservatives are ultimately right: The Bachelor, Joe Millionaire, Average Joe, My Big Fat Obnoxious Fiance and all the other "win a husband/wife" shows surely trivialize the sanctity of marriage and, in the process, turn straight coupling, for better or for worse, into pure entertainment. Heterosexuality never looked so fragile.

The Rise of Reality Marriage Shows

The breakthrough marriage show was ABC's The Bachelor, which debuted in 2002. In the interests of gender equality, the successful first season was soon followed by its matched set: The Bachelorette. These shows set up the bachelor/ette with twenty-five dates and allow him or her to eliminate a certain number each week until the number of potential mates has been winnowed down to four. At this stage, the lucky bachelor/ette meets the suitors' families and then makes a cut. When the suitors have been reduced to the more wieldy number of three, the bachelor/ette goes on intimate overnighters with each date (creating an adulterous scenario in the process). After another cut, the two remaining contestants meet the bachelor/ette's family, and then he or she makes a final decision and proposes on the season's finale.

The reality marriage shows actually replace family sitcoms about the drudgery and necessary hardship of marriage (Roseanne) and challenge other sitcoms about the fun of single life (Friends, Seinfeld, Sex and the City). By giving marriage a radical makeover, they revive the audience's interest in private lives and turn the viewer's attention away from the public sphere during a period of intense political secrecy, grotesque military blunders and faint public dissent. The marriage shows, like much reality TV, produce a steady stream of "real" images of "conflict" (Big Brother), "survival" (Survivor) and "terror" (Fear Factor), which then compete with real conflict, real survival and real terror.

But don't mistake me for a reality-TV basher. Ever the cultural optimist, I truly believe that audiences can read between the lines of pure ideology (romance) to see clearly the actual rendering of marriage in these shows as practical (tax credits, access to sex, state recognition, gifts at the wedding, gifts at the baby shower, social and familial approval), while at the same time understand real marriage as neither romantic nor practical (little access to sex after a while, expensive to have children, you hate each others' family and friends).

Superficial Soul Mate Searching

In the end, The Bachelor/ette openly depicts heterosexual mating patterns in a Darwinian, "survival of the cutest" way, in which men and women choose mates based on looks and immediate sexual chemistry alone. This turns heterosexuality into a highly superficial system of selection that runs counter to the ideology of romance manufactured by Hollywood and women's magazines—namely the "soul mate" model, which, in fact, most of the participants on these shows bring with them. All of the marriage seekers claim to be open to love and marriage; all tend to be young, good-looking and financially secure; many, weirdly, seem to be in "pharmaceutical sales" (you tell me). Most claim to have been either unlucky in love or just not managing to find that one special person. Meredith Phillips, for example, last season's [2003] "bachelorette," says she signed up for the show "in an attempt to find her soul mate." Meredith, a makeup artist and a model, was a participant on Bob Guiney's season of The Bachelor. When Bob picked another hopeful lovely from his batch of ladies, Meredith was crushed, since she had been sure that Bob was her "soul mate." But ABC allowed her another stab at tracking down the elusive "one and only," and the next season she claimed to have found him among the twenty-five financially secure prospective husbands picked out for her perusal. Soul-mate hunting, it turns out, depends less upon the twists and turns of fate and much more upon a well-funded boyfriend search on national TV.

A whole series of shows that followed The Bachelor, therefore, made it their mission to show that hetero men and women care about more than just money and looks. Average Joe, as the snappy title implies, asks a woman to choose from a set of "average guys," and Joe Millionaire has women compete for a guy whom they are tricked into thinking is very rich (in fact, he's a construction worker). While the goal of these parasite shows is to demonstrate that the participants really value relationships over fame, TV exposure, money and quick sexual encounters, in each case, greed and looks win out over other more abstract markers of compatibility. On Average Joe, for example, the producers send in a group of male models to confuse the bachelorette halfway through her process and, sure enough, each season, she jumps at one of the models and dumps the average Joes!

New Creative Lows

Reality shows, we now know, have a limited shelf life, in the sense that once the format has been learned by the audience, boredom can set in all too quickly. This season's The Bachelor, for instance, was so bad and so boring that you could not tell the difference between three out of the four final blonde women, and the fourth was cast as a psycho around whom the producers engineered a very halfhearted stalking episode.

The tedium factor drove all the networks to new creative lows this season, and they desperately fiddled with the format to try to find fresh arrangements of groomed male and female bodies in search of matrimony. So, audiences could

Four Christian Women Examine the Impact of Reality Marriage Shows

Reality television shows . . . have altered our . . . thoughts about romantic relationships. And while most of us are aware that shows such as The Bachelor, The Bachelorette, Joe Millionaire, For Love or Money, Blind Date, and ElimiDATE are mainly a form of entertainment, the word reality in this genre can be confusing. . . .

What messages do these shows send us about marriage?

LaTonya [Taylor]: On many of these shows, marriage is something women win. They earn it. They're good enough for it. I think that sends a damaging message to singles. It communicates, If you aren't married, you haven't won; you've lost. People often say, "Why isn't a pretty smart girl like you married?" as if it's a prize rather than a blessing that happens according to God's will and timetable.

Carla [Barnhill]: I think it's telling that none of these relationship-based reality shows has produced a lasting marriage yet.

Lisa [McMinn]: These shows send a warped image about love. The women claim to be in love after spending a few moments with someone. It's such a Hollywood notion of love, like love at first sight. What a misconception! In reality, love is based not only on attraction but on choice and commitment. Healthy relationships take time to grow and deepen. These shows give a shallow model of love, and it scares me that young girls are watching and being influenced by these messages.

Camerin Courtney, *Today's Christian Woman*, January/February 2004.

pick between My Big Fat Obnoxious Fiance, The Littlest Groom and even a gay show on Bravo, Boy Meets Boy. On the first, a woman has to trick her parents into accepting her "big fat obnoxious" fiance, who is played by a professional actor, in order to win a million dollars. In the second, a midget man picks between a group of female small people and some regular-sized women. And in the gay version, a clean-cut, handsome and smart white gay guy goes on dates with countless other clean-cut, handsome and smart white guys (only some of whom are actually gay) in search of a life partner. His challenge is to select the gay men from the gay impersonators. My Big Fat Blah, Blah, Blah failed because

the trickery was staged and blatant; the midget marriage series bombed because it exposed the "freak show" aspect of all
the marriage shows. And the "trick the fag" show ultimately
fell way short of its aspirations because the gay contestants,
in the end, seemed far more interested in cruising each other
than in focusing their attention on the one good-looking gay
guy selected by producers as the Prime Gay!

Reality Shows Ignore Interracial and Lesbian Dating

Two scenarios have so far been completely avoided by the
"get hitched in prime time" phenomenon. First, all the
shows have refused to test the waters of interracial dating,
and so far none have cast a bachelor/ette of color in the main
role. In a perfunctory nod to diversity, there are always contestants of color in the group of potential mates at the beginning of these shows. The black or Asian contestants usually
don't make it past the third round (you don't want to cut
them too quickly); the occasional ambiguous Latina/o can
make it a bit further. But in the end, these shows always manage to avoid parading interracial romance on prime time. A
suspicious viewer might be inclined to read intimations of
social engineering into these shows. Are they ads for white
families at a time when demographic shifts have made white
people a minority in certain cities and states? Are the shows
trying to caution against interracial unions or just portray a
process of "natural selection" as "color-blind"?

Second, while the format seems to extend to telegenic gay
dudes, so far there is no interest in creating a show about lesbian dating/mating. Far be it from me to advocate for such
a thing, given that, based upon The L Word, such a show
would undoubtedly involve hetero-looking bisexual babes
pressing up against each other for the viewing pleasures of
straight men. And yet, the absence of lesbians and people of
color (not to mention lesbians of color) bears mentioning.
Apparently, US audiences can thrill to the spectacle of arranged marriages and dating opportunities for all kinds of
white and heterosexual bodies, but the whiff of interracial or
lesbian trysts would make audiences queasy and stretch the
marriage paradigm to its limit.

On the finale of Average Joe Hawaii, one bachelor finally took a stand and rejected his new mate in a fit of pique. Was he reacting to the false moralism of the show? Was he refusing to fall in love in three days on national TV? Did he want to make a point about selling intimacy short? Nope, he was furious that his new girlfriend had held back from him a frightening secret: She had once dated [the actor] Fabio! Even though no one could explain why this "secret" should bother our "Above Average Joe," he claimed that "any guy in America" would feel as outraged as he did. What Fabio represented to this insecure model-actor we may never know, but these are the mysteries of reality TV that we must tolerate. In the end, our stud could not recover from this terrible disclosure, and the match made in NBC studios faltered and died a natural death.

Few of the hopefuls on reality marriage shows actually marry their new mates. Most use their time in the limelight to secure modeling contracts, get exposure as actors and enjoy the half-light of the semi-celebrity status that chases them for a few weeks after the show ends. Of course, if they were honest, the studs and babes would admit that the chance to nuzzle, cuddle and smooch twenty-five hotties with impunity in a two-month span is reason enough to sign on for the rocky ride of reality dating. But honesty is not the best policy for bachelor/ettes. So as each potential soul mate confesses to "falling for" (the most overused phrase in reality marriage land) the man or woman of the hour, the bachelor/ette returns the love and longing in equal measure and commits to love, honor and obey, forsaking all others, in sickness and in health, until death do they part, or at least until the next episode.

> *"People often seek out and enjoy the passivity, escape, and easy distraction that television viewing provides."*

Television Provides Escape

Robert Kubey

In the following viewpoint Robert Kubey claims that television serves a unique purpose: It provides a necessary distraction from the complexities of modern life. Dismissing predictions that computers and the Internet will soon make television obsolete, he argues that new media do not allow people to relax and escape from reality in the way that TV does. People crave simplicity, he contends, and TV offers uncomplicated escape. Robert Kubey is director of the Center for Media Studies at Rutgers University.

As you read, consider the following questions:

1. What factors influence television viewing habits, according to Kubey?
2. What is the author's response to George Gilder's prediction that TV will become irrelevant?
3. In Kubey's view, why do cable channels have a definite, memorable identity?

It's a safe bet that a fair amount of what is being currently predicted about the future of television, multimedia, and the Internet won't happen. Much forecasting about interactive television technology and computers involves the technological tail wagging the dog. "If it can be built, people will buy it," the developers think.

But the future rarely happens in the precise ways that the technoprognosticators predict. There will be a great many successful developments that no one forecast. This is the nature of technological development. As the television series *Connections* showed us, many great inventions are the result of planning and genius, but just as frequently they are the result of serendipity, luck, or accident.

Technophiles often miss the human factors, the individual and mass behavioral predilections that drive the adoption of new communication technologies.

Television viewing habits are substantially influenced by enduring features of how we live and when we go to work, how daily life is structured, even such factors such as how we respond to the weather. On any given weekday evening, for example, about one-third of the U.S. population is watching TV. In the winter when there is less daylight and people spend more time indoors, the fraction of the population watching television during prime time rises to one-half.

Work patterns dictate how much time people have available to be in contact with the leisure oriented media. While the world of work is currently undergoing considerable change, these patterns are not about to change radically for most people in the near future.

Unlikely Predictions for the Future of Television

More to the point, there are only so many hours in the day, a fact consistently lost on the technophiles and business interests that predicted and promoted the idea that we would all soon have 500 channels. Where is all the time and money going to come from to support 500 channels? And why was the number "500" so frequently bandied about in the first place? The very fact that so many people used such an incredibly round number should raise our suspicions as to how much thought, relatively little I would suggest, had really gone into such projections.

Consider what various so-called "experts" say and write. Andrew Lippman of the Media Lab at M.I.T., for example, wrote in a formal memo to Representative Edward Markey in 1994, "Forget television sets. In three years there won't be any. Instead, there will be computers with high-quality display screens." Nicholas Negroponte, director of the Media Lab, wrote, "The traditional 'mass media' will essentially disappear." George Gilder, in his book *Life After Television*, predicts a profound move toward high culture and a much more discriminating audience. He writes, "TV will be irrelevant in a world without channels, where you can always order exactly what you want when you want it. . . . All the media junk food and filler that stretches out toward the horizons of mass culture, like so much strip development, will tend to disappear."

People Do Not Seek Information of Value

The ideas that computers and the Internet will completely displace television, whether it be in the near future or even in a few decades, or that people will soon watch television very selectively and discriminately are very poorly founded in my view. As is Gilder's notion that consumers will precisely retrieve the information and entertainment that they want and that this will cause the disappearance of sensationalistic "media junk food." His view that people will become attracted to high culture and what he deems "valuable" information if only given the chance, is wishful thinking and in all likelihood, both naive and wrong.

Public and university libraries have long been reservoirs of information but how many people spend much time in the library or have ever even learned how to use a library well? Yes, the Internet offers enormously convenient access to much information, but if people were nearly so thirsty for information and books as Gilder claims, libraries would long ago have been packed.

Contemporary television technology does obviously allow for a great deal more discrimination in viewing than only 15 years ago but that hasn't meant that this potential is being taken advantage of in a manner congruent with Gilder's predictions. The vast majority of Americans now have cable and own a VCR, but how often do people use these innovations to plumb the depths of video information, entertainment, or film already available?

How People Will Use Technology Is Often Unpredictable

It's revealing that at conventions of video rental store operators, participants pass on the observation that tens of millions of U.S. homes contain VCRs that are blinking "12:00." Meaning, of course, that no one in the household has yet made the effort to learn to program the clock, and by extension no one in the household can program the VCR to tape asynchronously. A study by the Stanford Research Institute concluded that Movies On Demand, one of the interactive TV services thought to be most viable, would only attract two million customers over the first five years. Another study reports that only six percent of those who have ever bought pay-per-view prefer it to going to the video store.

These studies and stories serve as great palliatives for those in the video rental trade as it indicates to them that they don't have a great deal to fear at the coming of more pay-per-view and complicated digitized services. Most people still prefer to rent their videos from a store and bring them home. Precisely how many VCR programming-challenged people there actually are is an uncertainty, but I certainly know Ph.D.s and professors with computer backgrounds who have confided that they cannot, or have never learned to, program their VCR.

In short, people often do not use technology in the ways that the prognosticators would have us believe they will. On occasion, I've gotten sucked into a film being run on cable and watched it to its conclusion when I already had the film on tape nearby in the same room. I could have watched it any day over a number of years yet the tape sat solidly on the shelf never having been played. When it came on over the air or via cable, I began to watch.

I am not at all alone in this propensity to view less discriminately and to enjoy watching a program that is being televised in the here and now even when it's already available in one's

Television as a Diversion

The uses and gratifications theory is concerned with the way people use media in general, and television in particular. The objectives of uses and gratifications theory are (a) to explain how people use media to gratify their needs, (b) to understand motives for media behavior, and (c) to identify the functions or consequences that stem from needs, motives and behavior. One of the main assumptions of the uses and gratifications perspective is that media selection and use is purposive and motivated and that people take the initiative in selecting and using communication vehicles to satisfy felt needs and desires. Overall, the fact that consumers use media and specifically television purposefully in order to satisfy certain needs has long been supported by the uses and gratifications theory. . . .

Diversion refers to using media either as a form of escapism from real life situations or as a means to cultural gratification and entertainment. On one hand this means that viewers are bored or anxious and need a distraction to passively take their mind off things and relax, or "ritualized release" to actively divert themselves. On the other hand, by entertainment, viewers seek to satisfy their need for cultural or aesthetic enjoyment.

Research indicates that traditional TV use can be explained through the uses and gratifications perspective. Towards this direction, several studies have been carried out examining motives that the audience/user seeks to gratify while using television: entertainment, surveillance, escape, companionship, problem solving and personal identity.

Julia Livaditi et al., Proceedings of the 36th Hawaii International Conference on System Sciences, IEEE Computer Society, 2002.

video collection. Some people report that they like the fact that millions of others are watching the same program or film simultaneously, and of course this is especially true for live sports and breaking news. Suffice it to say that there is still a place for traditional television scheduling and mass dissemination even in the face of new superior communication and television delivery systems that some would have us believe are going to completely alter how we view. They won't.

Television as a Welcome Distraction

Much of my skepticism for the over-claiming about the future of interactive television is based on other researchers' work as well as my own. Reported in *Television and the Quality of Life*, written with Mihaly Csikszentmihalyi, is that people use television more for escape, and for entertainment and distraction, than for information gain. People often seek out and enjoy the passivity, escape, and easy distraction that television viewing provides.

They often want to "blob out." To be sure, they also enjoy interactivity in the form of video games, e-mail, and the Internet but by no means do they want to interact all the time, or even most of the time.

Though Time-Warner insists it was not a test of market viability and merely a $700 million experiment in technical feasibility, the company announced in May of 1997 that it would shut down its interactive television experiment in Orlando, Florida that included features such as banking, shopping, and movie ordering. As David Westin, president of production for Capital Cities/ABC Inc., has said, "People want to come home and relax and be entertained by their television set. They don't want to have to program it themselves."

Cable TV Is Becoming Too Complex

Research also indicates that people don't want 500 channels. Few cable viewers watch the majority of the 35–100 channels they already receive and most would prefer 30–40 channels that they like and that would permit them to pick from a smorgasbord of well-matched channel choices. But even then, research indicates that they would gravitate much of the time to five to seven favorites. This is why most cable channels have learned to define themselves with the fact in mind that viewers are most likely to keep returning to their preferred channels with a definite, memorable identity. Viewers want to know what they can expect from a channel whether it be CNN, C-SPAN, MTV, Nickelodeon, or BET. Except for those with very peculiar interests in television or who have scads of time, who needs 500 channels? And, of course, the simple economics of the situation preclude adequate financial support for hundreds and hundreds of channels. To assume that consumers will ratchet their price resistance levels ever upward is a mistake.

As early as May 1994, the *New York Times* was already reporting that the growth of new cable channels was slowing substantially because the number of available subscribers had begun to level off. Some industry analysts were predicting even then, that cable channels that reach "only" 20 to 30 million subscribers may be in substantial trouble. Thirty months later, the *Times* quoted industry analyst Marc Riely saying, "If you don't have the equity interest of a larger operator, or you aren't backed by a media company like Disney or Time-Warner, you'll have a really tough time getting launched." These economies of scale also explain why "niche" programming (e.g., jazz, ecology, Afro-Caribbean culture), some of which would be of special interest and value to various populations, is experiencing increasing problems finding cable systems that wish to carry it.

A related problem, seldom considered, is that there may be real limits on the amount of talent that can be brought together to make all the programs necessary to fill so many new channels. The industry already sees itself as being short on talent. [Comedy writer] Susan Harris reported to me during my research for my next book, *Creating Television: Then and Now*, that one summer she nearly jettisoned a new situation comedy pilot because she simply couldn't find an attractive, solid young male actor who could carry the lead in a comedy.

What the audience has always gotten from television, and what it will continue to want, is novelty and predictability simultaneously. Novelty in a safe context—in a box. Most fundamentally, that's what TV offers. Human beings only like to handle so much complexity and often prefer to simplify their worlds.

Periodical Bibliography

The following articles have been selected to supplement the diverse views presented in this chapter.

Andrew Collins — "Television: Entertainers or Social Workers?" *Observer*, February 20, 2000.

Camerin Courtney — "Romance, TV-Style: Four Women Speak Out About the Way Reality Shows Have Impacted Our View of Love and Marriage," *Today's Christian Woman*, January/February 2004.

Michael Goodspeed — "The Cultural Plague of Reality TV," Rense.com, April 15, 2004.

Ron Kaufman — "The Bachelorette 2004: The Reality of Television Escapism," Kill Your Television, 2004. www.TurnOffYourTV.com.

Chuck Klosterman — "Who You Callin' Normal?" *Esquire*, September 2004.

LimiTV, Inc. — "TV and Elementary Kids: Your Child's Brain Wasn't Built for All That TV," 2000. www.limitv.org.

Brian Lowry — "Obesity and TV: Lift That Remote, and Bend and . . . ," *Broadcasting & Cable*, June 28, 2004.

Rick Marin — "We're All Reality Stars," *USA Weekend*, February 15, 2004.

Media Awareness Network — "The Good Things About Television," 2005. www.media-awareness.ca.

Tara O'Gorman — "Soap Operas: Silliness or Escapism?" BellaOnline. www.bellaonline.com.

Wade Paulsen — "CBS Picks Up Mark Burnett's Controversial Child Rescue 'Recovery' Show for Midseason," Reality TV World, August 9, 2004. www.realitytvworld.com.

James Poniewozik — "Why Reality TV Is Good for Us," *Time*, February 17, 2003.

The Real Truth — "The Television Addiction, Part I," vol. 2, no. 3. www.realtruthmag.org.

Mary Ann Watson — "Ethics in Entertainment Television," *Journal of Popular Film and Television*, Winter 2004.

Susan Wloszczyna — "Ahead: Much Less Bang for Your Buck," *USA Today*, September 19, 2001.

Katrina Woznicki — "Experts Debate Media's Role in Obesity," United Press International, December 10, 2003.

CHAPTER 3

How Does Television Advertising Affect Society?

Chapter Preface

The average American child does not consume enough nutrients each day to meet the recommended nutrition guidelines set by the U.S. Department of Agriculture. For example, only 20 percent of children eat the suggested daily amount of fruits and vegetables. In addition, the American Association of Clinical Endocrinologists affirms that 25 percent of youths are obese, triple the number in 1980. As childhood obesity and malnutrition escalate, nutritionists struggle to pinpoint a cause, which will enable them to find a solution. Many experts are fingering TV commercials as the culprit. Some of the most heavily advertised items during children's television programs, they note, are foods, the majority of which are fast food, candy, and snacks high in fat, sugar, or salt. Many analysts attribute children's unhealthy eating habits to this barrage of junk food advertisements. Accordingly, several countries prohibit food commercials that target children. Restrictions placed on these advertisements raise serious questions about how television advertising affects viewers and how it should be regulated, if at all.

Some people feel that commercials promoting unhealthy foods to children are responsible for youths' declining health and thus should be banned. A 2001 study in the *Journal of the American Dietetic Association* found that only one or two exposures to a short food commercial can influence preschoolers' eating habits. The journal determined, "Preschool children's food preferences tended to reflect the television commercials they saw. Our results add to the body of literature showing that even brief exposure to commercials can influence children to choose low-nutrition junk food." Because young children are so easily persuaded by such advertisements, the researchers concluded, their exposure to food commercials should be limited.

Indeed, countries such as Sweden and Greece have imposed restrictions on food advertisements aimed at children, and the United Kingdom debated the issue in 2003. At the time the *Guardian* reported,

Options proposed by the [Food Standards Agency] include setting criteria for independent broadcasters on the "numbers and types of food adverts for less healthy foods to be shown during children's television." It also suggested banning food adverts aimed at pre-school children and restricting the use of children's TV presenters, cartoon characters and celebrities to persuade children to buy food that is high in sugar or salt.

Although the UK decided not to restrict TV advertising, child advocacy groups in the United States soon called for limits on commercials for foods that lack nutritional value. After exploring the role of the media in childhood obesity, the Kaiser Family Foundation, for instance, suggested removing food advertisements from children's media, including television.

Restricting food commercials, however, would certainly draw criticism from many analysts. Gerard J. Musante, founder of residential weight-loss facility Structure House, is among those who feel that efforts to outlaw the marketing of junk foods to children are misguided and counterproductive. Overweight people, he asserts, must take responsibility for their unhealthy lifestyles and should not fault advertisers: "The worst thing one can do is to blame an outside force. . . . No industry is to blame and should not be charged with solving [the] obesity problem." Lean O'Flaherty, senior nutritionist with the National Dairy Council, adds: "Obesity is a multifactorial condition. It would be very difficult to pinpoint something specifically in the diet and ban it. More avenues need to be explored before [banning food advertisements]."

Others who oppose restrictions on food marketing include advertisers, TV producers, and libertarians. Martin Paterson of the Food and Drink Federation believes that existing UK guidelines are adequate, and he rejects further restrictions. The guidelines, according to Paterson, "state that ads should not encourage children to eat or drink frequently throughout the day, condone excessive consumption, or suggest that confectionary or snacks should replace balanced meals." The food and drink industry has obeyed these regulations, he maintains, and should not be subjected to further restrictions. Television producers, too, protest bans on food commercials during children's programming because these would eliminate much-needed funding for children's shows.

Meanwhile, libertarians contend that marketers have a right to promote legal products, a right which would be violated by attempts to silence their messages.

Whether the government should prevent food advertisers from targeting children is clearly a thorny issue. At the center of the controversy is the question of whether or not television commercials can influence viewers. In the following chapter authors examine how television advertising affects society.

*"Alcohol advertising . . . will negatively
affect a population already at risk and will
contribute to an increase in stereotypical
misconceptions about alcohol consumption."*

Alcohol Commercials Are Detrimental to Society

National Council on Alcoholism and Drug Dependence

The National Council on Alcoholism and Drug Dependence (NCADD) fights alcoholism and other addictions as well as the stigmas associated with them. Alcohol abuse has deleterious effects, it maintains in the following viewpoint, and commercials promoting alcohol exacerbate them. The council is especially concerned that the liquor industry began airing commercials on a major network just after the September 11, 2001, terrorist attacks; it claims that people are more likely to abuse alcohol after such a trauma. Alcohol ads persuade citizens to start drinking, cause recovering alcoholics to relapse, and teach children that drinking is rewarding and free of consequences, charges the NCADD.

As you read, consider the following questions:

1. What requirements does Randy Falco say the liquor companies must meet before airing commercials on NBC?
2. In John Slade's contention, how might the alcohol industry be less self-serving?
3. Name the six conclusions of the Drug and Alcohol Abuse Prevention Committee's report.

National Council on Alcoholism and Drug Dependence, "Liquor Ads More than Just Bad Timing," www.ncadd.org, December 18, 2001. Copyright © 2001 by National Council on Alcoholism and Drug Dependence. Reproduced by permission.

For the first time since a voluntary liquor-industry ban against television commercials for alcoholic beverages was lifted in 1996, a major national television network has begun airing commercials for distilled spirits, or so-called hard liquor. In an effort to reverse a steep decline in revenue that has accelerated since [the] September 11th [2001, terrorist attacks], NBC, part of the General Electric Company, has agreed to air a multimillion-dollar ad campaign by the Guinness UDV division of Diageo. While the commercials must adhere to certain stipulations, "the timing couldn't be worse for those concerned with the devastating effects of alcoholism, one of the nation's most critical public health issues," says Stacia Murphy, President of the National Council on Alcoholism and Drug Dependence.

Persuasive Messages from Alcohol Companies

The first in a series of these commercials aired on Saturday, December 15, 2001, during NBC's popular comedy show "Saturday Night Live." According to Randy Falco, president for the NBC Television Network division of NBC in New York, the ads will follow "a pretty strict set of guidelines," including a requirement that the liquor makers must first run a four-month long series of social-responsibility messages on such subjects as designated drivers and drinking moderately before they can run commercials for their distilled-spirits brands. Nevertheless, according to Dr. John Slade, a professor specializing in addiction at the Robert Wood Johnson Medical School of the University of Medicine and Dentistry of New Jersey, "The alcoholic beverage industry seeks to increase its sales in the name of 'moderate drinking.' At the same time, it continues to make money by selling alcohol to heavy drinkers, to underage consumers, and to those whose drinking is acutely dangerous to themselves and others. The industry's professed interest in public health would be less self-serving if it promoted *moderate* drinking in parallel with effective efforts to reduce *immoderate* drinking." The tragic result is that many young people feel it is perfectly all right to get drunk, as long as they don't get behind the wheel of a car.

Alcoholism is a major public health issue in America. Alcohol abuse is the third ranking cause of death, exceeded only by

The Role of Advertising in Underage Drinking

The trends of an ever-increasing number of ads and continued overexposure of underage youth mark alcohol advertising on television from 2001 to 2003, according to a new analysis by the Center on Alcohol Marketing and Youth (CAMY):

- The number of ads increased each year, with an explosion of ads for distilled spirits on national cable networks leading the way: 298,054 alcohol ads ran on television in 2003, up from 289,381 in 2002 and 208,909 in 2001. Distilled spirits ads on cable networks grew from 513 in 2001 to 33,126 in 2003.

- With the continued increase of alcohol ads on television, the number of ads "overexposing" underage youth, ages 12 to 20, increased each year as well: 69,054 in 2003, up from 66,218 in 2002 and 51,084 in 2001. . . .

Public health research has found that youth exposure to alcohol advertising increases awareness of that advertising, which in turn influences young people's beliefs about drinking, intentions to drink, and drinking behavior. Brain imaging has revealed that, when shown alcoholic beverage advertisements, teens with alcohol use disorders have greater activity in areas of the brain previously linked to reward, desire, positive affect and episodic recall, with the degree of brain response highest in youths who consumed more drinks per month and reported greater desires to drink. The Federal Trade Commission (FTC) has noted that, "While many factors influence an underage person's drinking decisions, including among other things parents, peers, and the media, there is reason to believe that advertising plays a role."

Center on Alcohol Marketing and Youth, *Alcohol Advertising on Television, 2001 to 2003: More of the Same*, October 12, 2004. www.camy.org.

cancer and heart disease. It is linked to a broad range of societal problems such as crime, homelessness, family violence, teenage pregnancy, career dissolution and economic loss due to job absence, sickness and accidents. On top of this, as a nation, we can expect to see an increase in substance abuse directly related to the events of September 11th. As noted in a report by the National Center on Addiction and Substance Abuse at Columbia University (CASA), "Research demonstrates that exposure to trauma puts an individual at four to five times greater risk of substance abuse, and stress is considered the number one cause of relapse to alcohol and drug abuse. . . ."

In addition, adds Joseph A. Califano, Jr., CASA President and former U.S. Secretary of Health, Education and Welfare, "The Americans who are using drugs and alcohol to cope, or have relapsed from sobriety after the national tragedy, are the forgotten victims of September 11th. We must . . . be sensitive to the increased likelihood of substance abuse and relapse in the wake of the World Trade Center and Pentagon attacks."

Bad Timing

"Is now really the time for network television to start carrying ads for hard liquor? It's irresponsible," says Murphy. Well before the voluntary ban was lifted in 1996, alcohol advertising was known to have negative consequences. A January 1993 report by the Prevention Committee of Maryland Governor William Donald Schaefer's Drug and Alcohol Abuse Commission indicated that children's attitudes favorable to alcohol were significantly related to their exposure to alcohol advertisements. The research showed that when children's exposure to alcohol advertising increased, they: perceived drinking as more attractive, acceptable, and rewarding; viewed drinkers more positively; were more likely to believe that drinking is a way to relax and deal with stress; were more likely to agree that it's okay for teenagers to drink; were more likely to name alcohol than water as an appropriate beverage for adults; and had increased expectations to drink in the future. The research also showed that, for youth who already drink, exposure to advertising reinforced their drinking and contributed to higher levels of drinking. "Has anything changed since then?" says Murphy.

The National Council on Alcoholism and Drug Dependence is concerned that the alcohol advertising aired by NBC will negatively affect a population already at risk and will contribute to an increase in stereotypical misconceptions about alcohol consumption. [Murphy states] "We need to encourage Americans to drink less alcohol, not more; to educate the public that the use of alcohol, even in small amounts, can cause great harm. The only thing alcohol advertising does—beyond generating revenue for the alcohol companies—is to help support the myth that drinking is a risk-free activity."

> "*It is difficult to believe that Americans are a mindless herd of robots who will make a mad dash to their local liquor stores just because they see a few TV ads.*"

Alcohol Commercials Are Harmless

Adam Thierer

In 2001 NBC became the first national network in fifty years to air liquor commercials, sparking ire from those who claim that alcohol ads encourage alcohol abuse. In the following viewpoint Adam Thierer counters these assertions, offering evidence that exposure to alcohol advertising does not lead to increased alcohol consumption by adults or children. Furthermore, parents, not the government, he suggests, should be responsible for discouraging alcohol use among youths. In response to a proposed ban on liquor commercials, Thierer states that prohibiting alcohol advertising would violate the First Amendment by barring truthful speech about a lawful product. Adam Thierer is the director of telecommunications studies at the Cato Institute, a conservative think tank.

As you read, consider the following questions:
1. To what does Dr. Chafetz attribute claims by advocacy groups and the media that alcohol advertising encourages use?
2. What point does Doug Bandow make about the effect of advertising on youth?
3. In Thierer's opinion, how should readers respond to newspaper editorials advocating bans on liquor commercials?

If you've watched any television in your lifetime, chances are you've seen more than a few beer ads. In fact, some of the most memorable advertisements in the history of the medium have been produced by beer makers, as they vigorously compete for customer allegiance. It's just another part of doing business for beer companies, which depend on TV ads to build brand name recognition.

But if you're a consumer who enjoys other spirits besides beer, you might be wondering why you never hear anything on TV about your favorite brands, or even competing liquor products. The reason you do not is because, for the past 50 years, the spirits industry has lived under a voluntary ban on the placement of liquor ads on TV. But as revenues have declined gradually over the past two increasingly health-conscious decades, the industry has rethought the wisdom of the ban and began cautiously testing the regulatory climate by placing ads on some local TV or cable stations. The debate over the wisdom of this reversal has been heating up nationally since NBC announced [in 2001] that they would allow liquor commercials to run during late-evening programming, making them the first national network to do so.

Advertising Does Not Affect Alcohol Consumption Rates

Not surprisingly, a lot of social do-gooders are up in arms over this and are demanding that federal policymakers take action to halt the practice. NBC "is shirking its public interest responsibility as a broadcaster by putting its bottom line ahead of the health and safety of young people," says George A. Hacker, director of the Alcohol Policies Project at the Center for Science in the Public Interest. And Joseph Califano, director of the National Center on Addiction and Substance Abuse at Columbia University, told *The Wall Street Journal* [in December 2001], "The only solution now is for federal regulation, just as we have federal regulation prohibiting tobacco ads on television."

From a public policy perspective, the fear seems to be puritanical in character: If people see booze ads on TV, they will drink more. Such post hoc reasoning could be challenged on a number of grounds. Specifically, it is difficult to believe that Americans are a mindless herd of robots who will make a mad dash to their local liquor stores just because they see a few TV ads. In fact, Dr. Morris E. Chafetz, president of the Health Education Foundation and author of *The Tyranny of Experts*, argues that "the claim that advertising can lead anyone down the bottle-strewn garden path not only to drink alcohol but to abuse it, is pure hokum." In the mid-90s, Dr. Chafetz conducted a review of academic research for the *New England Journal of Medicine* on the question of how advertising affected alcohol use. His conclusion: "I did not find any studies that credibly connect advertising to increases in alcohol use (or abuse) or to young persons taking up drinking. The prevalence of reckless misinterpretation and misapplication of science allows advocacy groups and the media to stretch research findings to suit their preconceived positions."

Arguments Against Banning Liquor Commercials

So even though academic evidence suggests that exposure to advertising is unlikely to increase consumption, liquor companies are still willing to run ads, perhaps in an attempt to build brand recognition or attract beer and wine consumers. The question is, is there anything wrong with that?

The answer, of course, is all a matter of personal opinion. In a free society, however, people should be at liberty to make such choices without government entering the picture. Adults should be responsible for their decisions in this regard and they should exercise authority over their children until they reach an age when they can be trusted to make such decisions on their own. Employing the old "It's about the children!" defense to support an ad ban doesn't make sense for other reasons. As my Cato Institute colleague Doug Bandow noted in a 1997 *Wall Street Journal* editorial, "almost every good advertised on the airwaves may have some inadvertent adverse effect on the young," whether it is cars, riding mowers, high-fat food, or computers. "But that's no excuse for banning ads," concludes Bandow.

Moreover, children can see liquor ads in magazines and newspapers too, so should we ban liquor ads in print? Which raises another important question: Why is it that we con-

The Reality of Youths and Alcohol Commercials

Much has been made of the fact that many young people have greater recognition of some alcohol beverage brand labels than of former US presidents. These reports make great press but what does it all mean? Probably nothing because there is no evidence that such recognition leads to experimentation, consumption, or abuse. Sometimes it even appears to be related to less drinking later.

Similarly, most adults are probably much better at identifying photos of popular entertainers than of William Henry Harrison, Franklin Pierce, Chester Arthur, John Tyler, or other former presidents of the US. That probably doesn't mean much either. . . .

A widely reported "fact" is that by the age of 18, the typical young person will have seen 100,000 beer commercials. However, to see that many such commercials, it appears that a person would have to view television for about 161,290 hours or 18.4 years. Thus, a person would have to begin watching TV 24 hours a day, each and every day, from birth until after age 18.

In reality, viewers are much more likely to see alcohol portrayed during TV programs than during commercials. For example, an analysis of prime time TV found that alcohol commercials appeared at the rate of 0.2 per hour while drinking portrayals during programs occured 25 times more frequently, at five times per hour.

Perhaps those who want to reduce the presence of alcohol on television should propose eliminating the programming and let children watch commercials instead.

David J. Hanson, "Alcohol Advertising," Alcohol Problems & Solutions. www.Potsdam.edu.

tinue to tolerate an artificial regulatory distinction between print and electronic media? For decades, policymakers have imposed the equivalent of second-class citizenship on electronic media (television, radio) in terms of First Amendment protections. Unlike their print counterparts, which receive substantial free speech protections, electronic media face numerous speech restrictions that would be unthinkable for newspapers or magazines. So the next time you see a newspaper editorializing about the need to ban liquor ads on TV, fire off a letter to the editor and ask them how they'd feel about a federal ban on all those liquor ads that appear in the paper's pages and provide them with substantial revenues.

First Amendment Concerns

Anyway, a federal ban on televised liquor advertising would probably not pass First Amendment muster today. In the important 1996 decision *Liquormart, Inc. v. Rhode Island*, the Supreme Court struck down a Rhode Island ban on the advertisement of retail liquor prices outside of the place of sale since such a blanket prohibition against truthful speech about a lawful product betrayed the First Amendment. As Thomas A. Hemphill, a fiscal officer for the New Jersey Department of State, noted in *Regulation* magazine in 1998: "That landmark decision makes it much more difficult for legislators to restrict truthful commercial speech, thus establishing a precedent for more stringent evidentiary requirements underlying future advertising regulations. Therefore any new law that imposes a comprehensive ban on television or radio liquor commercials will probably not survive First Amendment judicial review." The Court bolstered this line of reasoning in the subsequent 1999 decision *Greater New Orleans Broadcasting Assn., Inc. v. United States*, which declared that the FCC [Federal Communications Commission] could not ban casino advertising in states where gambling was legal. The Court declared, "the speaker and the audience, not the Government, should be left to assess the value of accurate and nonmisleading information about lawful conduct." These decisions also suggest that the Court may finally be getting serious about affording commercial speech the same protections granted to political speech, a move that is long overdue.

A final concern about a federal regulatory response to TV ads relates to its potential applicability to the Internet. As television and the Internet increasingly converge and more Americans gain access to broadband connections, it is likely that more and more television programming will be made available over the Net. So any ban on liquor ads on TV would likely have threatening implications for Internet Webcasting in the long run.

In conclusion, there has never been any logic behind the artificial distinction between liquor and other products, such as beer and wine, when it comes to promotional activities. Alcohol is alcohol. Why should the form in which it is delivered change its legal status? And why place advertising restrictions on *lawful* products at all? If someone was trying to sell crack cocaine or cruise missiles on TV, it might make for a more interesting debate. But alcohol is a legal product that manufacturers have every right to promote. Policymakers need to take a sober look at these realities before they rush headlong into needless and unconstitutional restrictions on liquor advertisements on TV.

> *"The underlying fact is that no one really wants to see these commercials."*

Televised Prescription Drug Advertisements Are Indecent

Peter Bart

Prescription drug commercials are tasteless and shocking, argues Peter Bart in the following viewpoint. After examining television advertisements for pharmaceuticals created to combat impotence, he determines that they are wildly indecent and that few people benefit from them. While Bart acknowledges that pharmaceutical commercials cannot be prohibited, he implores networks to avoid airing them during dinnertime. Peter Bart is the editor-in-chief of *Variety*, an entertainment news source.

As you read, consider the following questions:

1. What leads the author to deduce that the pharmaceutical advertising wars are about to open a new front?
2. In Bart's contention, what happened after the government relaxed advertising regulations in 1997?
3. What is Levitra's slogan, as cited by the author?

Peter Bart, "Television Drug Blurbs: Ad Nauseam: Pharmaceutical Ads Promote 'Indecency' and Campaigns for Impotence Cures Make Things Worse," *Daily Variety*, vol. 283, May 3, 2004, p. 2. Copyright © 2004 by Variety Magazine, owned and published by Cahners Business Information, a division of Reed Elsevier, Inc. All rights reserved. Reproduced by permission.

E ver notice that when politicians talk about "indecency" in the media, they focus on shock jocks or edgy sitcoms? When ordinary viewers complain about tasteless TV, however, I find they're talking about those omnipresent drug commercials with their endless dissertations on hemorrhoids, bowel dysfunction, acid reflux and urinary leakage.

These ad onslaughts always seem to occur at meal time and are accompanied by obligatory recitations of potential side effects, which usually include hemorrhoids, bowel dysfunction, acid reflux and urinary leakage. Not to mention that most delightful of all symptoms—dementia.

I mention all this only because the pharmaceutical advertising wars are about to open a new front. More than $300 million has been earmarked by the three archenemies of impotence, and their campaigns aspire to new levels of shrill ubiquity.

The products involved are Levitra, Cialis and Viagra, and they're chasing what is projected to be a $6 billion-a-year market.

That's a big target. Get ready for the worst.

The Government Is Responsible for the Proliferation of Indecent Drug Commercials

Let me first remind you that it was our ever-protective government that initially unleashed the torrent of drug ads on us by reducing risk-warnings to a verbal blur. When the Food and Drug Administration relaxed ad regulations in 1997, the drug companies' TV ad spending tripled in two years to $2.5 billion.

Viewed from the standpoint of showbiz, the first generation of erectile advertising was only semi-excruciating. How can you relax in front of your TV set when a surly Mike Ditka is pointing a finger at you, as though you'd just dropped a pass?

Stuart Elliott, who covers Madison Avenue for the *New York Times*, assures us that the next generation of campaigns will be downright cool.

The Cialis commercials depict a couple relaxing in their bathtub—separate bathtubs actually—with the ominous question "Will he be ready?" The suggestion is that he'll be more than ready: Cialis claims to deliver a 36-hour window compared with the flaccid four-hour span offered by its two rivals.

With a promise like that, he'd better be ready.

Pfizer, which produces Viagra (still the market leader), has opted to emphasize the end results rather than the uneasy preparations.

Its new ads show a middle-aged man jumping for joy like an exultant third-grader as he's congratulated by co-workers. All the while "We Are the Champions" plays in the background like some sort of erectile anthem. The suggestion that satisfied Viagra users wander around their offices telling colleagues that they're now stand-up guys may strike some as far-fetched.

Seltzer. © by Parents Television Council, ParentsTV.org. Reproduced by permission.

Levitra is taking a less theatrical approach. "Quality when it counts" is its new slogan. This low-key message, says the company, will assuage those women who feel that "there are three people in bed—the man, the woman and the pill."

Irrespective of these tactics, all three products are still prescription drugs and hence must include the customary blurred warnings of headaches, heart attacks, panic attacks, etc. Most alarming is the admonition that if your appendage is still standing after four hours, you should immediately rush to the hospital—a stressful journey under the circumstances.

The Truth About Prescription Drug Advertising

No matter what artifices are introduced, the underlying fact is that no one really wants to see these commercials. The technicalities of male plumbing are about as unromantic as the list of side effects.

Indeed, the fusillade of new commercials will only underscore the dirty little secrets of the erection business.

For one thing, the real market for these products goes far beyond those poor souls suffering from impotence to all those young guys who regard these products as sex toys. Recreation represents the real upside of the business.

Sure, Viagra and its competitors may help some retirees who have given up on sex.

But think of all those nice old biddies who were perfectly happy to be post-coital and who joined the AARP [American Association of Retired Persons] because they thought it stood for the American Assn. of Retired Penises. Now along comes a product offering a 36-hour window? I can hear voices all over Sun City shouting, "Shut that damn window."

I realize there's no hope of banishing drug commercials, but can't the networks at least keep them away from dinnertime? There should be a safety zone when you'll be protected from talk of diarrhea, vaginitis—and 36-hour windows. Let the politicians fret about the shock jocks; at least the rest of us may have our moments of peace.

"Pharmaceutical advertising . . . prompts people to seek medical attention [and] promotes informed discussions with medical professionals."

Televised Prescription Drug Advertisements Serve a Public Need

Pharmaceutical Research and Manufacturers of America

The Pharmaceutical Research and Manufacturers of America (PhRMA) represents companies that develop new medicines. It asserts in the following viewpoint that commercials for prescription drugs benefit consumers by alerting them to diseases they may have and to available medications that may treat their conditions. Today's government regulations, the organization declares, ensure that prescription drug ads inform viewers about the drugs' risks. Additional advantages of pharmaceutical commercials, it contends, include encouraging patients to become involved in their own health care and fostering competition among drug companies.

As you read, consider the following questions:

1. In PhRMA's view, what was unsatisfactory about the regulation of pharmaceutical commercials before 1997?
2. What were the findings of *Parade* magazine's telephone survey, according to the authors?
3. How does PhRMA respond to claims that DTC advertising is driving up the cost of pharmaceuticals?

More than ever, patients are becoming involved in their own health destinies. The consumer movement and the information explosion have empowered patients to participate in decisions concerning their health care. Armed with information, patients have become active partners with health care professionals in managing their own health care —and they have become savvy consumers. Rather than remaining uninformed and relying entirely on health care professionals, patients today are asking questions, evaluating information, and making choices.

The sources of user-accessible information about health care have increased exponentially. Some 50 consumer magazines focusing on health care hit the news stands every month. Just about every television station in the country has a health care reporter dedicated to medical news. Internet users can surf tens of thousands of sites dedicated to various health care topics. The *Physician's Desk Reference*, or "PDR," once confined to doctors' offices, is now available in a consumer edition at pharmacy counters.

Direct-to-consumer [DTC] advertising enhances consumer knowledge about diseases and treatments. It also fosters competition among products, which can lead to improved quality and lower prices for consumers. Most importantly, direct-to-consumer advertising can improve public health. It helps start a dialogue between patients and doctors. Often, this dialogue will not result in the doctor prescribing the drug that the patient has asked about. But it will prompt a discussion that may lead to better understanding and treatment of the patient's condition. . . .

Since the early 1990s, pharmaceutical advertising has grown considerably and is today one of the fastest growing categories of advertising. In 1990, 10 different medicines were advertised directly to consumers. In 1997, that number climbed to 79 as the FDA [Food and Drug Administration] somewhat relaxed restrictions on DTC ads and as more pharmaceutical companies recognized the value in raising awareness levels of their medicines with patients.

In August 1997, the FDA issued proposed guidelines that clarified the agency's broadcast advertising (i.e., television and radio) requirements about a prescription drug's side effects. No longer would the FDA require ads to contain voluminous information about the drug's side effects in television and radio ads. Advertisements must still list major health risks and must include an 800 number, an Internet site or some other means for consumers to obtain information about side effects, such as a reference to a print advertisement. The agency has requested feedback on the proposed guidelines and will review comments before issuing final guidance [which it did in 1999].

The FDA's decision to clarify its regulations stemmed from a policy that led to ineffective and confusing advertisements. Prior to the 1997 guidelines, FDA regulations required that information on side effects, contraindications and other FDA-approved labeling information had to be included in all advertisements that both name a prescription drug and state its purpose. Pharmaceutical companies which wanted to include both the name of the drug and the condition it was meant to treat were forced to include reams of small print spelling out the FDA-required information. While feasible in newspapers and magazines, such ads were not suitable for radio or television.

This regulation prompted companies to advertise on television in more oblique ways, which, while meeting legal requirements, may have been less helpful to consumers. In such ads, either the name of the medicine or the name of the illness was mentioned—but not both. Consumers were often left to guess what the medicine was for.

This system was clearly unsatisfactory and the FDA clarified its requirements in the draft guidelines. As Dr. William Jacott, a trustee of the American Medical Association, said: "The problem with the way the FDA currently regulates ads is that they discourage companies from providing information that may educate the consumer. The merest mention of symptoms and a drug requires that a company also include reams of information that most people won't read and many wouldn't understand anyway."

Upon announcing the proposed guidance, FDA lead deputy commissioner Michael Friedman said: "Today's action can help promote greater consumer awareness of prescription drugs." And Robert Temple, associate director for

lical policy at the FDA's drug division, said that, under the
w guidelines, ads could inform consumers about new prod-
cts that they might not otherwise learn about. As an example, he cited a new generation of antihistamines that don't
cause drowsiness. "You need to be told by someone that those
products are out there or you'll never know," he said.

Consumers Benefit from DTC Advertising

A study released in May 1998 by *Prevention* magazine found
consumers give high marks to pharmaceutical advertising
because it "allows people to be more involved with their
health." Further, the study found that such advertising "is an
extremely effective means of promoting both the public
health and prescription medicines" and concluded that "the
benefits of DTC advertising could go far beyond simply
selling prescription medicines: these advertisements may
play a very real role in enhancing the public health."

A follow-up survey, released in September 1999, found
that 76 percent of adults think that direct-to-consumer advertising helps them be more involved in their own health
care and that 72 percent think direct-to-consumer advertising educates people about the risks and benefits of prescription medicines. In addition, the study found that this type of
advertising has a positive effect on compliance: 31 percent of
those who had seen an ad for their prescription medicine say
they are more likely to take the medicine, and 33 percent say
the ad reminded them to have the prescription filled.

The research determined that pharmaceutical advertising
has helped foster patient-physician dialogue where none had
previously existed and, more importantly, improved that dialogue as patients came prepared, armed with information
from websites, brochures and 800#s. In fact, the survey found
that direct-to-consumer advertising prompted an estimated
24.7 million Americans to talk to their doctors about a medical condition or illness they had never discussed with a
physician before. In other words, millions of people who had
previously suffered in silence were encouraged to seek help.

Other studies back up these conclusions. For example, in
telephone interviews with 1,500 adults conducted in May
1997, *Parade* magazine found that 73 percent agreed with the

statement, "Advertisements for prescription drug products have made me more knowledgeable of options available for treating ailments." And 72 percent of the *Wall Street Journal* subscribers surveyed in 1997 agreed that pharmaceutical companies should play an active role in informing consumers about medical conditions and possible treatments. In addition, 53 percent said that prescription drug advertising helps them better understand treatment options and that direct-to-consumer advertising is a necessary public service in today's health care environment.

Information That the Elderly Recalled from Prescription Drug Ads

	Recalled in All Cases (Percent)	Recalled In Some But Not All Cases (Percent)	Total (Percent)
A referral to a different source for more info	35.6	23.3	58.9
A Web site address or place on Internet	26.1	17.4	43.5
A toll-free 800 number	29.9	25.4	55.3
A statement about seeing a doctor	64.4	19.2	83.6
Warnings about side effects	63.9	11.1	75.0
Precautions against taking the drug	72.9	11.4	84.3
Warnings for people with illnesses	75.7	11.4	87.1

Anne Balazs et al., *Marketing in a Global Economy*, 2000.

In general, physician organizations have expressed concerns about direct-to-consumer advertising of prescription drugs, and polls of individual physicians reflect this point of view. However, a 1999 survey by Louis Harris Interactives and the Harvard University School of Public Health found a growing acceptance of direct-to-consumer advertising among doctors. According to Harris Poll Chairman Humphrey Taylor, "initially there was a sense of outrage among physicians [about direct-to-consumer advertising], and a feeling that only they ld talk to patients about prescription drugs," but doctors easingly recognize the benefits of these ads. The poll and that 49 percent of physicians believe direct-to-consumer dvertising of prescription drugs had helped "educate and inform" their patients, and one-quarter of the physicians surveyed believe that the ads have increased patient compliance.

Criticism of DTC Advertising

Critics of DTC advertising claim that it drives up pharmaceutical expenditures. In fact, total pharmaceutical expenditures are increasing, due primarily to greater use of new and better medicines by more patients. This increased utilization reflects the extraordinary value that medicines provide, to patients and to the health care system. Increased utilization of medicines is a good thing—it helps many patients get well quicker and avoid hospitalization, surgery, nursing home admission and other, more costly forms of care.

Another criticism is that DTC advertising misleads consumers into believing they need drugs that may be inappropriate for them. In fact, while DTC ads prompt patients to consult their physicians about available medicines, the doctor still holds the prescribing pen. Patients cannot get prescription medicines unless their physicians find that the medicines are necessary and appropriate.

Pharmaceutical Advertising Can Improve the Public's Health

PhRMA [Pharmaceutical Research and Manufacturers of America] believes that advertising directly to consumers serves to improve public health. As patients are participating more and more in decisions concerning their health care, pharmaceutical advertising helps meet consumer demand for information about health conditions and possible treatments. Often, this information prompts people to seek medical attention, promotes informed discussions with medical professionals and further enhances the dialogue between physicians and their patients. Since prescription drugs are available only under a doctor's supervision, there is little danger that advertising will lead to inappropriate use. Instead, it will prompt informed discussions between patients and physicians that may lead to better treatments.

Pharmaceutical advertisements raise awareness of conditions and diseases that often go undiagnosed and untreated. Further, such advertising can raise awareness that treatments are available to populations that have traditionally been undertreated. According to the American Diabetes Association, for example, there are 6 million Americans with diabetes who don't know they have the disease. One third of the people with major depression seek no treatment, and millions of Americans are estimated to have high blood pressure and don't know about it. By informing people about the symptoms of such diseases and the availability of effective treatments, direct-to-consumer advertising can improve public well-being.

There are encouraging signs that DTC advertising is getting more people diagnosed and treated. For example, in the two years that ads for a medicine for erectile dysfunction have appeared, millions of men have visited their doctors to request a prescription for the drug. For every million men who asked for the medicine, it was discovered that an estimated 30,000 had untreated diabetes, 140,000 had untreated high blood pressure, and 50,000 had untreated heart disease. And, according to a study by IMS Health, in the one year after an advertising campaign for an osteoporosis drug began, physician visits for women concerned about osteoporosis doubled.

Consumers are actively seeking information about their health and about medicines. Pharmaceutical companies are a prime source of such information. Patients have the right to ask for information about the treatments available, and the companies that develop those treatments have a right to communicate information about these problems and about health problems to patients.

riodical Bibliography

The following articles have been selected to supplement the diverse views presented in this chapter.

Council	*Public Service Advertising That Changed a Nation*, September 2004. www.adcouncil.org.
Doug Bandow	"Advertising and Alcohol," Cato Institute, October 6, 1999. www.cato.org.
Center on Alcohol Marketing and Youth	*Alcohol Advertising on Television, 2001 to 2003: More of the Same*, October 12, 2004. www.camy.org.
Rance Crain	"Take Me Out to the Ball Game, If Only to Escape Fox Promos," *Advertising Age*, November 4, 2002.
Erwin Ephron	"The Long Goodbye: Are We Already Living the Death of TV?" *MEDIA WEEK*, April 26, 2004.
Richard Frank et al.	"Trends in Direct-to-Consumer Advertising of Prescription Drugs," Kaiser Family Foundation, February 2002. www.kff.org.
Harry A. Jessell	"Commercial Overload," *Broadcasting & Cable*, November 6, 2000.
Jeffrey Krauss	"DVR/PVR Threats and Opportunities," *CED (Communications Engineering & Design)*, November 2004.
Kyle McCory	"Crusading Against Alcohol," *Daily Titan*, May 20, 2003.
Tom Reichert	"Sexy Ads Target Young Adults," *USA Today (Magazine)*, May 2001.
Chris Sprigman	"Are Personal Video Recorders, Such as ReplayTV and TiVo, Copyright-Infringement Devices?: A Lawsuit Raising the Question May Force SonicBlue to Spy on PVR Users," FindLaw, May 9, 2002. www.findlaw.com.
Mukul Verma	"Zap TV: Advertising Will Morph as More People Use Cheap Digital Recorders to Skip Commericals," *Greater Baton Rouge Business Report*, January 6, 2004.
Janet Woodcock	"Statement Before the Senate Special Committee on Aging," July 22, 2003. www.fda.gov.

CHAPTER 4

How Should Television Be Regulated?

,pter Preface

e United States broadcasters that televise indecency or anity between 6 A.M. and 10 P.M. can be fined $27,500 by Federal Communications Commission (FCC). Yet when .usician Bono uttered the f-word during the live 2003 ;olden Globe Awards, the FCC declined to penalize TV networks that aired the unexpected profanity. Outraged Americans complained that punishments for televised indecency are not issued often enough and are too lenient. In response politicians introduced the Broadcast Decency Enforcement Act of 2004, which would have increased maximum fines for obscenity on public airwaves to $500,000. Efforts to rally support for stricter regulation of television were challenged, though, by those who believed that vulgarity is protected by the First Amendment and should not be limited. The controversy over whether the government should punish networks for airing indecency is just one segment of the debate over whether and to what extent television should be regulated.

Broadcasters have a right to express any viewpoint, conceded the drafters of the Broadcast Decency Enforcement Act, but they also have a legal and moral duty to shield viewers from obscene content. Congressman John D. Dingell, who supported the bill, explained, "Our constituents are fed up with the level of sex and violence on television and radio, as well as with the Federal Communications Commission's lax attitude regarding indecency complaints." According to some proponents of the bill, the lack of enforcement and relatively small fines for violations encourage networks to air more sex and fouler language. An appropriate response, maintained Kansas senator Sam Brownback, is to increase fines. He put the numbers into perspective:

> [$500,000] seems like a lot of money. However, compare that to the fact that a 30 second commercial during the 2004 Super Bowl cost advertisers an average of $2.3 million. In the words of FCC Commissioner Michael Powell, these fines are 'peanuts' to these big media conglomerates.

Responding to claims that the Broadcast Decency Enforcement Act would violate the free expression rights of entertainers and broadcasters, representative Christopher Cox declared, "This is not about free speech. This is about decent speech." In his view, obscenity on public airwaves is not constitutionally protected.

Free speech advocates, however, disagreed with the conclusions of Cox and other supporters of the act. Their main objection was that the FCC's definition of indecency as "patently offensive sexual or excretory references" is too vague, and if fines for violators were to be increased to half a million dollars, broadcasters would censor all views or actions that could be perceived as inappropriate. Even educational programming, suggested opponents of the bill, would be subject to heavy fines. Journalist Thane Peterson used the example of *Saving Private Ryan*, an acclaimed movie about soldiers in combat that many stations pulled from their prime-time lineup on Veteran's Day 2004 for fear that its violence and use of the f-word might warrant sanctions from the FCC. Peterson contended, "My worry is that the legitimate concerns about violent, smutty, vapid fare on TV will be used to launch a jihad [holy war] against worthy programming." He also criticized the FCC for throwing out its indecency guidelines in 2004, which "explicitly said the full frontal nudity in *Schindler's List* [a movie about the Holocaust] was acceptable because of its 'manner of presentation' and because it was in historical context." The FCC, lacking specific guidelines for what constitutes indecency and armed with the Broadcast Decency Enforcement Act, could force stations into financial ruin for airing certain educational programming, free speech advocates charge.

By the close of 2004 the Senate and House had been unable to reach a compromise regarding the bill. However, when the Broadcast Decency Enforcement Act was reintroduced in 2005, proposing to fine TV networks $500,000 and entertainers an additional $500,000 for each instance of obscenity, the House passed the act and at press time the Senate was considering it. The heated debate over whether and how indecency should be regulated—and how it should be defined—illustrates the contentiousness of the issue of television regulation. Whether Congress can agree on a law that shields viewers from vulgar material while alleviating free speech concerns is yet to be seen.

> "The [Federal Communications] Commission currently receives thousands of indecency complaints every day, yet acts on only a handful."

Indecency on Broadcast Networks Must Be Restricted

Eva Arlia

In the viewpoint that follows, Eva Arlia declares that the government must heed the public's calls to restrict the indecency, vulgarity, and other immoral behavior that she says pervade television. The Federal Communications Commission (FCC), she charges, does not adequately enforce decency laws. It must levy larger fines against all networks that broadcast obscenity, Arlia maintains. Eva Arlia is an intern with Concerned Women for America (CWA), which aims to bring Biblical principles to all levels of public policy.

As you read, consider the following questions:

1. According to Arlia, what is the number two rated television show in the United States?
2. What action does the author say the CWA took in April of 2003?
3. In Janice Crouse's opinion, what will happen if America does not clean up its culture?

S ince the 2004 presidential election, the nation has been abuzz with the increased influence of "morality" in the voting preferences of Americans. Eleven states voted to reject homosexual "marriage," Florida denied abortion for minors without parental notification, and gambling initiatives were repeatedly struck down.

Why is this so surprising?

Perhaps it is because, at first glance, one may not guess that we are a moral nation. Look at the TV shows, the music, the movies that we consume for entertainment. The recent trend in politics does not reflect the spiraling culture in which we find ourselves.

Dr. Janice Crouse, senior fellow of the Beverly LaHaye Institute, added, "We have also learned from recent polling that 20–30 percent of the so-called values voters watch the television shows; they go to the movies; they read the magazines and they listen to the music. Increasingly, secularism is having more influence on Christians than Christians are having on the secular world."

Television Is Offensive

For the past decade, the hottest phenomena in media have featured sex, vulgarity and other forms of lewdness. Currently, ABC's *Desperate Housewives* is the new "it" program. Based in modern-day wealthy suburbia, the characters include: Susan Mayer, a divorcée and single mother who seduces a neighbor; Lynette Scavo, stay-at-home mom of four who uses her children's attention deficit disorder medication to keep her own life on an even keel; Bree Van De Kamp, a mother who loses complete control of her family and attempts to murder her husband when he proposes divorce; and Gabrielle Solis, a bored wife who finds excitement in an affair with her 17-year-old gardener. . . .

The American public is eating it up. It is now the number two show on TV. Critics say that it is a wonderful, behind-the-scenes view of suburbia, addressing "the updated and eternal myth of momhood," [according to writer Ellen Goodman].

Consider a second case: ABC sank to new lows again with another drama series, *Life as We Know it*. This time targeted at the teen audience and airing on Thursday nights at 9 P.M., this show tells the story of three hormone-charged teenage boys and their obsession with sexual fantasies and desires. Dino Whitman, Ben Connor, and Jonathan Fields are all "utterly consumed by thoughts of girls" (one with his English teacher), and the show portrays their relationships with each other and those around them as they are "shaped into men," [reads its plot synopsis on ABC's Web site].

Countless more examples of songs, movies and TV shows persuade the public to believe that greed, lust and dishonesty are "normal." The next generation is getting these messages from our media.

The Need for Better Regulation

Outrage over these types of shows is widespread. Concerned Women for America (CWA) and other grassroots organizations have organized massive campaigns against indecency, shedding light on the lack of regulation surrounding our media.

In April of 2003, CWA experts joined a coalition of family groups that met with three of the five commissioners of the Federal Communications Commission (FCC) and urged them to take action and strongly enforce indecency violations. In addition, CWA backed the preservation of broadcast decency language in the Department of Defense Authorization bill in September, increasing FCC fines to $275,000 per offense. Congress will again address this issue when the Broadcast Decency Enforcement Act is re-introduced in the 109th Congress.[1]

Regrettably, the FCC has not been as effective as CWA hopes in fighting indecency. The Commission currently receives thousands of indecency complaints every day, yet acts on only a handful. In 2003, for example, citizens lodged more than 202,000 complaints, but just three notices of apparent liability (NALs) were issued to broadcasters for indecency violations, totaling less than $450,000. Only one of those three notices has been paid [as of November 2004].

FCC Commissioner Michael Copps stated in a December

---

1. As of early 2005, the bill had passed in the House and was expected to reach the Senate shortly.

Pushing for a Strict Definition of Indecency

We [the Federal Communications Commission] do have a statute that we're supposed to be enforcing against indecency, and most especially for the protection of children during the hours when they are most likely to be tuned into [network TV]. But we are doing a woefully bad—I believe—job of implementing that statute. I think there was one instance of a fine against a station last year [2001] that actually went all the way to collecting the fine. That's just simply inadequate.

We have to look at what is the solution to that. If it is the definition of indecency that the Commission has developed, then we need to be thinking about a new definition. Although I must say, had we been really serious about our enforcement responsibilities, we could have brought a lot of things to closure and to fines and to sanctions using the definition that's already there. But if that's not going to work, then we need one that doesn't let so many things get through the cracks. I have proposed that in the last several weeks [of 2002] to my colleagues. . . .

I would not be prepared to say exactly what that definition should look like. I would like to have a public notice, and a formal proceeding, saying "We are looking for and considering a new definition of indecency," and I would like everybody on all sides of the question to chime in—those who want stringent enforcement, the First Amendment people, all the various cause groups and advocacy groups. Then we can take the best of the insights and the best of the thoughts that we get in and craft something that will pass muster, and that will be workable, and that will be effective in getting the job done—and is presently going undone.

I would add to that when we are looking at that new definition, I would think that we ought to incorporate the factor of violence, as well as sexually explicit material, in that definition.

Michael J. Copps, interviewed by Morality in Media, December 4, 2002. www.moralityinmedia.org.

2002 interview: "It's not a credible enforcement process. If you're going to have a credible enforcement process, you have to have punishments, and those punishments have to exact a toll."

Dr. Crouse adds, "Until we get serious about cleaning up American culture, our airwaves and the broader entertainment industry will continue to pollute our children's minds and corrupt the overall society.". . .

Though the situation in American media appears dismal, we must not slow down. Our continued resolve will include applying pressure on those who perpetrate indecency and harm our youth. We will continue to lobby the FCC for stronger enforcement standards, so that our complaints and voices will be heard. Let us "fight the good fight of faith" (1 Timothy 6:12) and stand strong to return our nation to its moral roots.

"It no longer makes sense to apply one set of rules to broadcast and an entirely different set of rules (or no rules at all!) to cable."

Indecency on Cable Networks Must Be Restricted

Parents Television Council

The Parents Television Council (PTC) works with government and television officials to set and enforce broadcast decency standards that limit sex, violence, and profanity on television. It claims in the following viewpoint that millions of parents subscribe to cable TV so that their children can access wholesome, educational programming not available on broadcast networks, yet these cable packages also include channels that air obscene material. To help parents protect their children from graphic content, the government should regulate cable TV, asserts the PTC. The government should either grant the Federal Communications Commission (FCC) the power to fine cable networks that air indecency or require cable companies to allow consumers to receive and pay for only the stations they want, the PTC suggests.

As you read, consider the following questions:

1. Why should the FCC be lauded, in the PTC's opinion?
2. In the author's contention, how is cable TV accelerating the descent of broadcast TV?
3. The PTC asserts that the f-word is spoken how many times in *South Park the Movie: Bigger, Longer, and Uncut*?

Parents Television Council, "Basic Cable Awash in Raunch," www.parentstv.org, November 2004. Copyright © 2004 by Parents Television Council. Reproduced by permission.

"It's tough to get that sexual point of view across on television. Hopefully I have made it possible for somebody on broadcast television to do a rear-entry scene in three years. Maybe that will be my legacy."

—Ryan Murphy, Creator of the
pornographic FX series *Nip/Tuck*

In 2003 the Parents Television Council released a series of studies on the State of the Television Industry. Those reports showed that sex, foul language, and violence on broadcast television are not only more prevalent today than ever before—such content is becoming far more explicit. Under mounting pressure from an angry public, in 2004, the Federal Communications Commission (FCC) finally started to crack down on indecent television broadcasts. In fact, the FCC issued more fines for televised indecency in 2004 than in the entire previous history of the agency.

The FCC should be lauded for finally addressing this long-standing problem. Parents can be optimistic that fear of penalties or license forfeitures will encourage the broadcast networks to clean-up their acts, but will it make any difference in the long run if indecent content is still rampant on basic cable?

The Rise of Cable TV

Cable began as an alternate television service to households where reception of over-the-air TV signals was poor, and has since expanded into a multi-billion dollar industry. Between traditional cable service and satellite television, most basic cable channels reach upwards of 85% of Americans, making advertiser-supported basic cable nearly as pervasive as broadcast television.

With so little family programming available on the broadcast networks, it's no surprise that millions of parents choose to subscribe to some kind of basic cable package in order to gain access to wholesome and educational programming available on a handful of cable networks. But to access these networks, parents are also forced to pay for channels they don't want and that actually make their job as a parent much more difficult. Now, in addition to trying to protect their children from the filth on Fox, NBC, UPN, and the other broadcast networks, they also have to try to protect their children from the much more explicit fare on MTV, FX, Comedy Central, and the like.

Children are watching these programs and are being exposed to content that is far more explicit and potentially far more damaging than what they are seeing on broadcast television.

Cable TV is also helping to accelerate broadcast TV's descent into the sewer. Network executives frequently cite competition from cable as a justification for pushing broadcast standards down. The statement above by Ryan Murphy is no idle threat. It is a reflection of a pattern we've seen repeated time and again. Once basic cable programmers are able to break down advertisers' aversion to sponsoring explicit language, or graphic sex and violence, there's no longer an obstacle to getting an advertiser to underwrite the same kind of content on broadcast television.

Government Regulation

In today's media environment, it no longer makes sense to apply one set of rules to broadcast and an entirely different set of rules (or no rules at all!) to cable. Either the FCC must start looking at cable indecency, and fining the stations and cable carriers that violate decency standards, or consumers need to be given the option of buying their cable packages on an à la carte basis.

It is unconscionable for the cable industry to force families to subsidize this kind of filth for the privilege of being able to watch TV Land, or the Food Network, or Disney Channel. Parents should not have to pay for programming that undermines their core values and beliefs.

Offering parents the ability to choose the channels they want, and to pay only for those channels, puts power back in the hands of the consumer and forces the producers of indecent or violent programming to fund their own raunch. These morally degrading networks have been carried on the backs of American consumers long enough. It is time for this extortion to end.

The following examples are taken from a broad range of cable channels that are part of most basic or expanded basic cable packages. The programs listed below aired during all times of day, from early in the afternoon to late at night. . . .

South Park—Comedy Central 06/20/2001
Cartman: "Tonight, on Cop Drama, on TV, they're gonna say shit."
Kyle: "They're gonna say shit on television?"
Stan: "You can't say shit on television!"
Cartman: "People are freaking out, dude."
Stan: "Holy [bleeped . . .] shit."

South Park the Movie: Bigger, Longer, and Uncut—Comedy Central 10/23/04
Comedy Central has aired this R-rated movie several times, unedited. The film, which only narrowly avoided an NC-17 rating by the MPAA [Motion Picture Association of America], contains over 130 uses of [the f-word]. . . .

Nudity and Sex on Cable TV

Anna Nicole Show—E! 9/8/02
Anna and her assistant Kimmy are watching the Chippendale dancers. A stripper unzips his pants and turns so his backside faces the audience. He is wearing a thong and his naked buttocks are blurred. The stripper is pulling his thong down and the full buttocks are blurred. He is now nude. Another stripper is dancing seductively in front of Anna while she drinks her champagne and rubs his chest.
Anna: "There was a male strip club in Texas and, um, they were doing dances for us, the girls, and I just love to have males dancing around. It really makes me hot."
One naked stripper is shown pouring water on himself. His buttocks are blurred also. . . .
One of the strippers pulls Anna on stage. They sit her in a chair and sing a song for her. A man (dressed as an electrician or plumber) begins dancing in front of her. He places her hands on his buttocks and continues dancing. Another stripper places Anna's hands on her chest and jiggles her breasts.
Anna: "We wasn't tired so we wanted to go see some girl strippers. So we went to this new club called Jaguars." Anna dances with a pole (like the strippers) because the strippers

Regulation of Indecency on Cable May Be Constitutional

[In March 2005], many were shocked that Senate Commerce Committee Chairman Ted Stevens (R–Alaska) pronounced that he intended to apply broadcast indecency standards to cable and satellite television/radio. [Columnist and former TV critic] Jeff Jarvis called the scheme "abhorrently unconstitutional." Others may also be under the impression that broadcast television and radio is unique in being subject to much less First Amendment protection than other media and that cable/satellite would be protected. I disagree. I think it is quite possible to draft constitutional satellite/cable indecency regulation. From Reuters:

> Stevens disputed assertions by the cable industry that Congress cannot impose limits on its content. "If that's the issue they want to take on, we'll take it on and let the Supreme Court decide."

Stevens may well be right. . . .

Herewith, my first-draft proposed language to regulate cable/satellite indecency:

> (a) Whoever utters any obscene, indecent, or profane language by means of radio or cable service shall be fined under this title or imprisoned not more than two years, or both.
> (b) A multichannel video programming distributor shall not be liable under this section for channels primarily dedicated to sexually-oriented programming.

Now, my analysis of why this may be constitutional.

The first part of the proposed statute's language is very clearly based on [a U.S. law], which gives the FCC authorization to set fines for broadcasting indecent language over the air. If [the code] is constitutional, then the only question is whether the addition of the words "or cable service" would render the statute unconstitutional. If it did it would have to be because cable service and radio broadcast are sufficiently different according to a constitutional analysis. I don't think they are.

Ernest Miller, "Regulation of Indecency on Cable/Satellite May Be Constitutional," Corante, March 7, 2005. www.corante.com.

---

asked her to. One stripper's bare chest is shown, but it is blurred.

Kimmy is receiving a lap dance from one of the strippers. The stripper's bare chest is blurred. Kimmy rubs the woman's thigh and grabs onto it. Another stripper is bouncing up and down on Kimmy's lap while Kimmy slaps her buttocks. . . .

Real World XII: Las Vegas—MTV 9/24/02

Trishelle begins a sexual relationship with housemate Steven on only their second day in the house. In a camera confessional, her roommate Brynn complains about having to listen to Trishelle and Steven being intimate in the next bed, but adds that she wouldn't mind partaking in some activity with both of them. Later in the episode, the housemates are all out at a club together. Brynn, Trishelle, and Steven are all intoxicated. On the dance floor of the club, Brynn and Trishelle kiss passionately. Later that night, they return to the house and the three of them are in a hot tub together, the girls in skimpy bikinis, Steve in swimming trunks. The three of them are kissing, touching, and fondling one another. Later, the activity moves to the bedroom. Trishelle, wearing only a towel, is in bed with Steven who is also wearing only a towel. Brynn goes into the room and climbs on top of them in bed. One of the girls can be heard saying, "Oh, my gosh! This is so naked!"

> *"You cannot legislate . . . decency in a society where half the population is offended by the F-word and naked bodies, and the other half spends billions of dollars on adult entertainment."*

Televised Indecency Should Not Be Censored

Joe Saltzman

Joe Saltzman is a journalism professor and associate mass media editor of *USA Today*. In the following viewpoint he maintains that it is absurd to restrict indecency on television under the guise of protecting youth. Reminding readers that indecency is purely subjective, he asserts that activities labeled as indecent by some people are enjoyed by much of the population. Saltzman also faults claims that children must be protected from obscene content, pointing out that nudity and profanity are not inherently offensive to children—they learn from adults that these behaviors are taboo. Furthermore, he reasons, it is ridiculous to censor profanity on television when it can be heard anywhere in America.

As you read, consider the following questions:

1. In Saltzman's contention, why does Congress hold hearings on indecency?
2. When does censorship become fashionable, in the author's view?
3. When discussing the uproar over the 2004 Super Bowl halftime show, what point does Saltzman make about the violence of football?

Joe Saltzman, "Why Can't You Say—or Show—That on TV?" *USA Today*, vol. 132, May 2004, p. 75. Copyright © 2004 by the Society for the Advancement of Education. Reproduced by permission.

E ach election year, whenever the economy and the deficit become major issues, Americans are dying on foreign soil, and there is a health-care crisis that overwhelms the social fabric, it is guaranteed that Congress will hold hearings concerning sex and/or violence on television.

Forget the highest deficit in the country's history, the millions of Americans who cannot get adequate health care, and the men and women dying [while fighting a war] in Iraq. Let's worry about the new buzzword—indecency. Focus instead on an 18-frame glimpse of Janet Jackson's breast[1] or fret about a common F-word being used (in a nonsexual way) [by U2's Bono] during an awards ceremony, or cringe because our neighbors may be seeing something on television that is offensive to other decent human beings.

Profanity and Tastelessness in America

It may come as a surprise to some representatives that the notorious F-word and all of its variations probably is the most common form of expression throughout the country after "the," "a," and "is." Go into any barbershop, beauty salon, fire or police station, construction site, junior high school, college dormitory, bar and grill, drugstore, supermarket—any place people gather, including freeways and public events —and that word constantly will be floating through the air. There even are American subcultures whose jargon is arranged around colorful variations of it. It is as much a part of their verbal repertoire and thought process as any adjective, verb, or noun.

Yet, Congress is alarmed that it might be heard on the airwaves, offending every innocent in the audience, especially children. Never forget the children. An adult sounds silly when bemoaning partial nudity or an expletive. Yet, when that same person couples the complaint with a plea for the children, it becomes fashionable. Censorship may be a word that alarms many Americans, but not when used in conjunction with kids. We must protect our impressionable youth from the language and images that are upsetting to a small

1. During the 2004 Super Bowl halftime show, which aired live, performer Janet Jackson's breast was briefly revealed.

percentage of the adult populace. Why rude expressions and pictures involving the human body are taboo is an issue that probably never will be resolved. Those who consider the television controversy absurd drama realize that, to many citizens, it is the beginning of the end of civilized society.

Sexuality Is Overcensored on Television

[In 2004], Channel 13 [in New York] killed a spot for the acclaimed movie "Kinsey," in which Liam Neeson stars as the pioneering Indiana University sex researcher who first let Americans know that nonmarital sex is a national pastime, that women have orgasms too and that masturbation and homosexuality do not lead to insanity. At first WNET said it had killed the spot because it was "too commercial and too provocative.". . . [Soon] the "Kinsey" distributor, Fox Searchlight, let the press see an e-mail from a National Public Broadcasting media manager stating that the real problem was "the content of this movie" and "controversial press re: groups speaking out against the movie/subject matter" that might bring "viewer complaints.". . .

[Because] of "Kinsey," the Traditional Values Coalition has called for a yearlong boycott of all movies released by Fox. (With the hypocrisy we've come to expect, it does not ask its members to boycott Fox's corporate sibling in the Murdoch empire, Fox News.) But such organizations don't really care about "Kinsey"—an art-house picture that, however well reviewed or Oscar-nominated, will be seen by a relatively small audience, mostly in blue states [which tend to vote Democratic]. The film is just this month's handy pretext for advancing the larger goal of pushing sex of all nonbiblical kinds back into the closet and undermining any scientific findings, whether circa 1948 or 2004, that might challenge fundamentalist sexual orthodoxy.

Frank Rich, *New York Times*, December 12, 2004.

The uproar during the Super Bowl halftime concert and the subsequent fallout over the viewing of Jackson's breast does not seem to make any sense when you talk about taste and decency. For example, what is tasteful about a commercial played during the Super Bowl broadcast in which a horse lifts his tail to deliver a burst of flatulence that explodes in a woman's face; or children with bars of soap in their mouths because, when they see a cool, new car, they yell "Holy S . . .";

or, for that matter, 22 men who will do anything and every-thing to stop the other team from scoring—with close-ups of blood flowing from one player's nose, another writhing in pain after being gang-tackled, and the quarterback lying prone after yet another vicious sack. What kind of society tolerates that type of tastelessness, then labels a brief glimpse of a female breast indecent?

Indecency Is Purely Subjective

Kids are among the most tolerant people around. They do not realize that nudity or profanity is offensive until adults tell them. They love everything about the human body that most grown-ups find tasteless and disgusting—burping, farting, vomiting, and anything involving snot. Children's authors know this very well. Maybe that explains why a best-selling children's book concerns a farting dog. Many of these youngsters grow up to be adults who continue to laugh shamelessly at juvenile jokes about bodily functions.

The bottom line is that what is objectionable to one person may not be to another. You cannot legislate taste or even decency in a society where half the population is offended by the F-word and naked bodies, and the other half spends billions of dollars on adult entertainment. The definition of what is tasteful and decent and what is not becomes tangled in a person's culture, vocabulary, and peer approval.

To add to the confusion, how do you define indecency when four of the most critically acclaimed series on television—"Sex and the City," "The Sopranos," "Six Feet Under," and "Curb Your Enthusiasm"—not only win the industry's top awards and make the "Top 10" lists of most TV critics, but also use the F-word, sexual content, and nudity repeatedly? Who decides what is indecent, and does it really matter?

Congress Needs a Distraction from Larger Social Problems

Congress does not care about any of this. It knows that a large percentage of the voting public is outraged when children are exposed to what they deem indecent language or images. Hearings on indecency give the appearance of doing something—even if it is not in any way relevant to the real problems facing the country. Congress understands full well that the budget deficit is here to stay; there is no possibility of universal health care this year; and Americans will be dying in Iraq throughout 2004. Hearings are a wonderful distraction. Politicians have known since the days of the Roman Empire that bread and circuses will keep an angry populace at bay. So bring on the circus. Legislators are hoping that the public focus can be shifted to the F-word and naked bosoms—at least until the November [2004] elections are over and business can go back to normal.

*"The horror of war can be portrayed
without gratuitous images."*

War Footage Must Sometimes Be Censored

Chris Cramer

Chris Cramer, president of CNN International Networks, wrote the following viewpoint two weeks after Operation Iraqi Freedom began in March 2003. In it, he attests that terrifying, graphic war coverage sometimes must be censored and that journalists should be especially sensitive in wartime. News footage must be edited to shield viewers from grotesque scenes of war, he maintains. Moreover, he stresses that broadcasts should be delayed to allow military officials time to inform the friends and family of injured soldiers before they see news coverage of their loved ones. Delaying live coverage also gives stations time to verify information and review reports that could harm national security, Cramer asserts.

As you read, consider the following questions:

1. When did CNN almost delay a live news report during the war, according to Cramer?
2. In the author's view, what effect did Al-Jazeera's broadcast of gruesome war coverage have on newsrooms around the world?
3. What was the benefit in waiting to air the videos of people captured by Iraqi insurgents, in Cramer's opinion?

We're over two weeks into the war in Iraq and I have many more grey hairs than I did at the start. The consolation is that I'm not the only one.

News broadcasters around the world are struggling with a new set of ethical and journalistic issues as they continue to provide 24-hour coverage.

The first week showed that the latest technology, and the co-operation of the US and British military, could deliver memorable live coverage of what looks the fiercest ground war since World War II. But with it came the potential of terrifying trench warfare and tank battles and the real likelihood of death and injury in front of our eyes.

This enhanced coverage poses a dilemma: how to weigh any editorial value in broadcasting death in a war against the tragic reality of that carnage on the screen, especially as live transmission may be picked up by the friends and families of those being filmed.

Live Video Delays Can Be Advantageous

Many broadcasters, including CNN, have the capacity to delay live video to air, normally to avoid abusive callers on phone-ins. Now we have put the same technology in place to give us an override button if our live coverage becomes too gruesome. We came very close to that point when live interviews were interrupted by "incoming fire", and during terrifying footage of intense fire fights in places like Umm Qasr [Iraq]. More recently, we actually used video delay on live reports from CNN correspondent Walter Rodgers as he travelled with US forces towards Baghdad [Iraq].

I know some of our critics will say that such interruptions or delays can only be due to editors distorting the truth for sinister political ends. But the conflict in Iraq has made a new generation of television editors face up to the problem that while the range of images empowers them, it also places huge responsibilities on their shoulders. One "embedded" reporter has already drawn criticism after a bizarre display on live TV in which he sketched the battle plan in the sand in front of US viewers.

Scenes like this highlight both the advantages and the disadvantages of continuous TV news. Can it generate more "heat" than "light"? Do we engage in a pinball game in which we bounce from one live event to another, rarely pausing to point up the significance and the context?

There have been times in the past few weeks [in spring 2003] when the enormity of the events unfolding, frequently live, on our screens has overwhelmed the most experienced TV editors and newsroom managers.

Polls Show Most Americans Believe the Media Should Be Restricted During Wartime

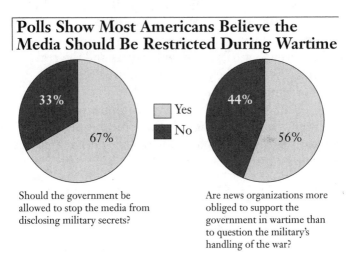

Should the government be allowed to stop the media from disclosing military secrets?

Are news organizations more obliged to support the government in wartime than to question the military's handling of the war?

Compiled by the book editor using statistics from an ABC News poll, January 16, 2003.

Our critics rushed to judgement in the first week of the war when some Arab TV stations, including the widely available Al-Jazeera, ran lengthy interrogations of five US prisoners of war together with gruesome video of the bodies of others, some apparently after execution. Their decision to broadcast in full, without any prior warning, meant newsrooms around the world were faced with not just having to juggle the editorial imperative with the feelings of the families involved, but also cultural, political and censorship issues.

Some broadcasters ignored what most of us believe is the first principle of TV journalism: that just throwing material on the air without bothering to examine its veracity is an abdication of our duty. Others, like CNN and the BBC, decided against such knee-jerk broadcasting. We gave time in the US and UK for families to be informed. We edited out the more gruesome parts of the material. And then we broadcast it. We lost nothing in the process.

Just 24 hours later, broadcasters were tested again with the release of footage that showed, apparently, the mutilated bodies of two British soldiers, together with two men claimed by some to be British POWs [prisoners of war]. After due pause we decided to obscure the dead soldiers' faces and transmit this image.

As for the so-called "POWs", our instincts told us that soldiers are rarely captured in civilian clothing, and never have long hair. We held the pictures until we were able to determine that they were, in fact, aid workers.

Good Journalism Omits Gratuitous Images

In the week [since], our decisions have centred on appropriate coverage of civilian casualties. Once again, some Arab TV stations decided to show endless, unedited pictures of the dead and injured. Broadcasters like CNN and the BBC have long believed that the horror of war can be portrayed without gratuitous images, but our critics accuse us of censorship and add that this is not simply an issue of professional ethics but more one of culture. Audiences in the Arab world and elsewhere, they argue, are more used to seeing these images and apparently less sensitive. And none of us should overlook the risks that many Arab journalists are taking to bring the story to their audiences.

Either way, there is no textbook for covering the events in Iraq. Broadcast news editors will often need to make snap judgements based on experience and instinct. They could do well to heed the words of a BBC editor covering the troubles in Northern Ireland in the 1970s. He said that broadcast news "must reserve the right to shock the audience . . . and use it sparingly."

I believe that editorial integrity is never defined by how many gratuitous images can be transmitted, or how much breaking news we can all throw on to air. The audience deserves and expects better. I think we will be judged on the quality of the journalism, the accuracy, the sensitivity and the tone. Only on that basis will we be able to assess if we have met the challenges of the first live TV war.

> *"Networks [won't] show their viewers the [war] images that will repel and revulse even the most hardened hawks."*

War Footage Is Too Sanitized

Gwen Lister

Gwen Lister is founder of the *Namibian* newspaper; in 2001 she was named one of the 50 World Press Freedom Heroes. In the following viewpoint she accuses U.S. television networks of presenting a one-sided view of the 2003 Iraq war in order to maintain public support for it. For example, she claims, U.S. networks tend to show the humanitarian efforts of soldiers rather than airing footage of traumatic bombings. What's more, Lister reports, live news coverage of the war is often inaccurate because journalists are not skeptical enough of U.S. sources and neglect to fully investigate events before airing footage of them.

As you read, consider the following questions:

1. In Lister's contention, what image do embedded journalists put forth?
2. Which three examples does the author use to support her claim that journalists lack skepticism towards news sources?
3. What do TV networks show in their "sanitized" version of the Iraq war, according to Lister?

It is undoubtedly fascinating and even mesmerizing to watch war, live on television. But I am conscious, as I'm sure are many other viewers the world over, that we're largely seeing, on these channels, only what "they" want us to see. It is the sanitized version. Nothing too ugly, so the undiscerning viewer may think, and even believe, that [Operation Iraqi Freedom] is a worthy war that is all but won.

Manipulation of the TV News

The reality is somethimg totally different and, if you're lucky, and equally perceptive, you might catch a glimpse of it coming through now and then on your television screen: the traumatized and bleeding face of a child visible in a bombed building; a petrified dog fleeing as a missile is fired from a U.S. gun emplacement. Generally speaking, though, we're simply seeing the relentless war machine hammer away at Iraq, from the air and the land and the sea. And we are seeing the talking heads sitting in the comfort of Camp David or 10 Downing Street [where the British prime minister resides], spouting off their moralistic propaganda about securing world safety and winning the fight on weapons of mass destruction.

But the United States networks in particular, and to a lesser degree the British, prove that they're not going to show their viewers the images that will repel and revulse even the most hardened hawks. So the some 500 "embedded" journalists largely put out the image that the respective military forces and their political masters want the world to see.

[President] George W. Bush, according to White House spokesperson Ari Fleischer, "doesn't really watch TV." As if we believe that! This U.S. President, who himself ducked service in Vietnam, now finds it all too easy to wage war and probably revels in the images.

The media are manipulable, particularly the vast TV networks. CNN, to our surprise, went against a Pentagon recommendation that they not screen the faces of POW's [prisoners of war] or bodies of U.S. soldiers, for that matter. It is clear that while the public . . . is generally amenable and supportive of the war effort, the tide can turn if and when enough U.S. casualties are reported. And they don't want to lose public support in this war of all wars.

Misinformation and Exaggerations

The BBC's Mark Damazer has already admitted that reporting of allied military claims in Iraq that later proved false—such as the heralding of the fall of Um Quasr [Iraq] at least nine times—had "left the public feeling less well-informed than it should be." He agreed, too, that language used was misleading, such as claims of an area in Iraq being "liberated." "That's a mistake," he said. "The secret is attribution, qualification and skepticism," he added, a sentiment expressed by a U.S. media-monitoring group, Fairness and Accuracy in Reporting.

The News Must Show War as It Really Is

We don't show the faces of the dead. We don't show the faces of the wounded, especially in this time of satellite television. We don't want to be in a position where we on television are notifying the next of kin. But I think you do show bodies, shooting them in as responsible a fashion as possible. In time of war we don't want to soft-pedal what is going on here. That would be contrary to the whole purpose of our being here. One thing you cannot do is leave people with the impression that war is not a terrible thing.

Ted Koppel, quoted in Howard Kurtz, *Washington Post*, March 28, 2003.

Fairness and Accuracy in Reporting openly criticizes the networks, in particular, for a lack of skepticism towards official U.S. sources who had already led journalists into embarrassing errors in their Iraq coverage. Among others, they've claimed the Iraqis have fired Scuds (subsequently denied by military sources). (It is also worth recording that despite being touted as the prime raison d'etre for the war, no weapons of mass destruction have either been found in Iraq or used by the Iraqis in the conflict.) TV journalists even discovered a chemical plant that in fact did not exist!

Reference even to "coalition forces" is stretching the truth. It is simply the United States, the British allies, the Australians, and a few Polish noncombatants. For the rest, there is no real "coalition." The language of the networks in this regard speaks volumes. It is evident that objective journalism has been lost in the "us" and "them" scenario, in which Iraq is openly referred to as "the enemy."

The United States as an Occupier

George W. Bush is getting muddled, too, but the networks won't point this out. First he promised a short war, then he said it would be longer than anticipated, and so it goes. But no one points out these discrepancies. The TV networks generally show the sanitized version of the war. Iraqi civilians smiling as they're treated for war wounds in a hospital; military medical corps operating to save the lives of "enemy" soldiers; distribution of food and water—and so it goes. And much of the unsuspecting public is probably totally taken in by these images, and most of the U.S. public still appear to fervently believe that their troops are "liberators" rather than the occupiers they really are! (The raising of the U.S. flag at Um Quasr was a revealing "mistake.")

There's no truth in the propaganda that the United States wants to give Iraq back to the Iraqis. Simply put, they want it themselves. Already a U.S.-based company has been given the multi-million dollar task of managing the Um Quasr port. This is reality TV with a huge slice of Hollywood. So watch with this in mind and, where possible, turn to alternative sources of information, because fortunately those who haven't been jammed or taken off the Internet or bombed off the face of the earth by the United States are still out there.

> *"The purpose of ownership restriction in communications law—originally for radio, later TV—was to avoid an over-concentration of the sources of news."*

Broadcast Ownership Limits Are Necessary

Lionel Van Deerlin

In the following viewpoint Lionel Van Deerlin, former chairman of the House Subcommittee on Communications, argues that media monopolies are dangerous and therefore ownership restrictions are necessary. He examines the Sinclair Broadcast Group, which just before the 2004 elections planned to air a documentary criticizing presidential candidate John Kerry on sixty-two stations. Van Deerlin expresses concern that Sinclair's biased message would reach 25 percent of U.S. homes. Broadcast ownership laws were formed, Van Deerlin avers, to ensure that viewers could receive information from many media outlets, yet he charges that a few networks—and their views —dominate television. After Van Deerlin and others objected to the documentary, parts of it were shown on forty channels but it was not aired in its entirety.

As you read, consider the following questions:

1. What does Van Deerlin say is strange about the FCC's claim that it cannot prevent the broadcast of the Kerry documentary on sixty-two stations?
2. In the author's opinion, how have Michael Powell and the FCC allowed concentration of the media?

A merica's biggest chain owner of television stations has perpetrated an outrage which, if tried 25 years ago, would have put it out of business. Days before a national election, all 62 stations owned or operated by the Sinclair Broadcast Group are airing a "documentary" sharply critical of Democratic nominee John Kerry.

The content of the program—whether or not it accurately portrays one of the major party candidates for president—is of only secondary concern. What's happening here tells more than some may wish to know about the way certain industry operatives get their way with government. Ancient Romans called it quid pro quo—something for something.

The chairman of the Federal Communications Commission issues a statement declaring his regulatory body powerless to halt the mass mugging of candidate Kerry. Presumably, our No. 1 overseer of the airwaves has not even considered urging Sinclair's wayward management to ponder its responsibilities under the law.

This seems strange, inasmuch as the FCC's job is to award broadcast licenses, and to monitor their use "in the public interest, convenience and necessity" (as the Communications Act has required since 1936).

But it could be that Chairman Michael Powell, son of the [former] secretary of state, feels no urge to dissuade these biggest of all broadcasters from doing precisely what they wish. Powell and his commission majority have been willing spear-carriers in an industry power grab comparable to Teapot Dome[1]—and carrying a much higher price tag. They have approved merger after grasping merger. Broadcast licenses which once were limited to seven per owner—a restriction that applied even to the networks—are now concentrated in the hands of ever-fewer owners.

The purpose of ownership restriction in communications law—originally for radio, later TV—was to avoid an overconcentration of the sources of news and opinion. Sinclair's far-flung properties (mainly in the East and Midwest, with Sacramento's KOVR-TV the chain's only California outlet) are said to penetrate one of every four U.S. homes. Only the

1. Teapot Dome was an oil-reserve scandal in the 1920s.

Hearst newspaper chain[2] in its heyday ever approached that reach.

In addition to the cash cow it enjoys by government franchise, Sinclair ownership takes full advantage of the political clout accompanying its access to a quarter of the country. In nearly 100 U.S. communities, the editorial policy of a major broadcaster is determined not through judgments reached locally, but by the thinking of a corporate headquarters many miles away.

Siers. © 2000 by North America Syndicate. Reproduced by permission.

With its unprecedented last-minute campaign splash—beyond any administration's expectation, we should hope—deregulation of the airwaves comes full circle. This is not a Michael Moore film booked into movie theaters, which we can choose to patronize or not. It is a slanted message whisked to viewers by a government licensee who doubtless hopes his political kiss-kiss will help him gain and dominate even more broadcast outlets.

The scramble to acquire licenses had begun before the

2. William Randolph Hearst, who published the *San Francisco Examiner* and the *New York Journal*, owned more than thirty newspapers in 1922.

present administration reached Washington. But the trafficking in broadcast properties has since seen the intensity of an Oklahoma land rush. Nor is it cynical to take note of some huge campaign contributions on record from Sinclair corporate officials, directed almost exclusively to the party in power.

And now, as yet further quid pro quo, hundreds of thousands of dollars worth of election-eve TV time on 62 stations. Ninety minutes of free advertising for the Bush campaign, uninterrupted by commercial breaks.

Needless to report, this had not met universal approval within the chain's clientele, some of whom are less enthralled than Sinclair management with prospects of a second Bush term. Business protests and ad cancellations have resulted, most recently in left-leaning Madison, Wis.

Sinclair's most laughable defense of the impending telecast was that it would deal with legitimate news—to wit, that it examines the upset feeling many Vietnam veterans still harbor over Kerry's anti-war activities in the closing days of the Vietnam struggle.

News? To ease a corporate conscience, perhaps, these TV toadies next "invited" the senator to take part in a question-and-answer session on all stations airing the hit film. The condemned's last words, we might suppose, immediately following his execution.

Attorneys for the Democratic National Committee and the Kerry campaign have done what's expected of lawyers— filed objections with the FCC and Federal Election Commission.[3]

As well they should. But the offense in question turns on something in our democracy which is badly broken—on an impropriety so gross that the sleaziest CEO must know what he's doing.

---

3. The Federal Communications Commission declared that it could not interfere with the broadcasting of the documentary. The Federal Election Commission was unable to respond to the complaint before the November 2004 election, which Kerry lost.

"Mergers are not in and of themselves bad. People forget that monopoly isn't even illegal."

Broadcast Ownership Limits Are Unfair

Michael Powell, interviewed by Drew Clark, Nick Gillespie, and Jesse Walker

Antitrust laws were enacted by the government to promote competition, encourage diversity, and prevent monopolies. While Michael Powell was chairman of the Federal Communications Commission (FCC), he favored loosening regulations for TV broadcasters and allowed broadcasters to merge into what some people call monopolies. According to Powell, he did so because he believes that the media is already quite diverse and that antitrust laws are unevenly applied in the area of media ownership, unjustly targeting TV network owners. In the following viewpoint he explains to *Reason* magazine that the government unfairly restricts how much of the national audience a TV broadcaster can reach but does not impose similar limitations on cable or satellite TV providers. Raising the limit for broadcasters, he claims, would neither cause the media to become too concentrated nor affect diversity of news and opinions.

As you read, consider the following questions:
1. Who does Powell claim is in charge of setting media ownership limits?
2. To what can people's fear over media monopolies be attributed, according to Powell?

Michael Powell, interviewed by Drew Clark, Nick Gillespie, and Jesse Walker, "The Reluctant Planner," *Reason*, December 2004. Copyright © 2004 by the Reason Foundation, 3415 S. Sepulveda Blvd., Suite 400, Los Angeles, CA 90034, www.reason.com. Reproduced by permission.

Reason: Let's [discuss] the very political issue of the media ownership rules.

Powell: We're not talking about media ownership. We're talking about broadcast ownership. I'm troubled by the continued approach in which media that are extremely competitive with each other—media that compete for news, information, resources—are nonetheless cut up and categorized differently and then get entirely different regulatory regimes.

Limitations on Broadcast Networks

Can you give a quick example?

Powell: One of the biggest firestorms was over this national cap [on what percentage of the national television audience a single owner can reach], whether it was 35 percent [the former cap], 45 percent as we suggested, or 39 percent, which Congress picked. Going to 45 percent means maybe one to two more stations per network in the United States. That's all that means. So a broadcast network is only allowed to reach with its product 45 percent of America.

But why can cable reach 100 percent? Satellite television can reach 100 percent. The Internet reaches 100-plus, if you want to go outside the U.S.

So why 45 percent? Why not 46 percent? Why not 100 percent?

Powell: This is where it's not just an academic argument. If Congress wants, as the 535 representatives of the American public, to say we're going to draw a limit, they can draw a limit. They can delegate that authority to an institution like this one [the Federal Communications Commission], whose duty it is to follow the limit. And no matter what my personal view is, I'm not going to debate whether there should be a limit.

If Clear Channel [Communications] suddenly owns six, seven, or, under a different regime, a dozen radio stations within the same market, is that something people should worry about?

Powell: Yeah, absolutely. It's something the commission worried about. It's rarely reported, but we tightened the radio rules. I hate when people describe my views as laissez faire [the belief that government should not interfere in economics], because I don't think there's any such thing. Capitalism would not work without the rule of law, and it would not work without certain understandings about rules and limitations.

I'm an antitrust lawyer. I completely accept that concentration at some measurable level becomes anti-competitive and harmful to the American consumer.

The Effects of Monopoly

Can you give an example of that?

Powell: There's Standard Oil [which dominated the industry for decades].

Most of the revisionist histories of Standard Oil show that by the time it had its maximum market penetration, it was actually charging less for oil.

Powell: You may know more about the specifics of Standard Oil than I. But I do believe in the cases and the theories that show that at a certain level of monopolistic control people can extract monopoly rents and affect output in a way that harms the American consumer.

Media Diversity Regulations Are No Longer Necessary

The FCC implemented its media diversity rules at a time when few [media options] existed. . . . Cable television channels [had not yet] proliferated into the three-digit inventory we now have available. Likewise, even major cities lacked the dozens of broadcast radio and television outlets now available in medium and small cities.

[At that time,] 90 percent of people watching television viewed only one of three major networks, whether by choice or due to the lack of available options. . . .

The scarcity of options justified regulation, and now in most instances the proliferation of options justifies streamlined regulation.

Rob Frieden, *Newsday*, May 21, 2003.

I think the United States, more than any other nation in the world, has got antitrust right. The presumption is business is OK. The presumption is mergers are not in and of themselves bad. People forget that monopoly isn't even illegal. The only thing we're looking for is whether the monopoly actually causes anti-competitive effects that are measurable on consumers. I've worked at the antitrust division. I've seen cases where we believed unequivocally that it did. You can find them. You could find the price increases, you can find the data that would demonstrate that and that you needed to do something about it.

But in media, it's less than that. If all we were doing is measuring concentration in the traditional way [by evaluating how much of the market is owned by one firm], we all know how to do that. I could decide whether Clear Channel is too big on concentration and anti-competitive grounds, but the argument in the country is not that. Something far short of that should be a "no" on diversity grounds [that is, if the broadcaster is not too concentrated and anticompetitive, it cannot be said to reduce product diversity]. . . .

The Broadcast Ownership Debate Is Founded in Fear

Do you think there's any principled way to determine the right levels of diversity and localism[1]?

Powell: At the end of the day you have to do something that you're comfortable with, but you have to accept a big margin of error. What are you trying to achieve with localism? Issues relevant to their community and not just issues relevant to the nation and the world are part and parcel of what's covered by properties that are licensed in the public interest.

I can pull public records and look at programming choices and what percentage of local news is on vs. five years ago, and I can measure it. We did all of this in the media ownership proceeding, and the reason I am a little saddened by what happened is that the work in there is phenomenal. We had data that never existed before. We found things to measure that . . . are indicative of a good story, and things that were indicative of a bad story.

What do you think accounted for the firestorm over the ownership rules?

Powell: It's because this is an extraordinarily media-intense

1. the responsiveness of a broadcast network to the needs of its local community

culture. Getting your voice heard is a source of both pleasure and aggravation.

The debate is more of a stalking horse for a general anxiety about media's role in our daily lives than it is about the rules. It became symbolic in an era where there was deep anxiety about globalization, a deep anxiety about corporate America. And the rise of things like Fox, which is the first network with a more conservative element in it. There's a whole 'nother constituency that thinks that's the problem.

Periodical Bibliography

The following articles have been selected to supplement the diverse views presented in this chapter.

Julia Angwin and Matthew Rose	"When the News Is Gruesome, What's Too Graphic?" *Wall Street Journal*, April 1, 2004.
G. Beato	"Drowning in Decency," *Rake*, May 2004. www.rakemag.com.
L. Brent Bozell III	"It's Time for Cable Choices," Creators Syndicate, April 8, 2004. www.parentstv.org.
Michael J. Copps, interviewed by Morality in Media	"Copps: 'Widespread Popular Revulsion' with TV Programming; Indecency Standard Should Be Revisited," December 4, 2002. www.moralityinmedia.org.
Rob Frieden	"FCC Should Loosen Media Ownership Rules," *Newsday*, May 21, 2003.
Mark Hirsch	"Self-Censoring in the Newsroom," *Broadcasting & Cable*, June 21, 2004.
Ron Kaufman	"The Boob Tube," Parts 1 and 2, TV Turnoff Network, 2004. www.turnoffyourtv.com.
Rami G. Khouri	"Getting a More Complete War Story," *Daily Star (Beirut, Lebanon)*, March 25, 2003. www.nieman.harvard.edu.
Paul Klite	"TV News and the Culture of Violence," Rocky Mountain Media Watch, May 24, 1999. www.bigmedia.org.
Ernest Miller	"Regulation of Indecency on Cable/Satellite May Be Constitutional," Corante, March 7, 2005. www.corante.com.
James Poniewozik	"The Decency Police," *Time*, March 20, 2005.
Deborah Potter	"Impressive but Incomplete," *American Journalism Review*, May 2003. www.newslab.org.
Michael K. Powell	"New Rules, Old Rhetoric," *New York Times*, July 28, 2003.
Norman Solomon	"Why the FCC's Rules Matter," *Birmingham Weekly*, June 5, 2003.
Adam Thierer	"Parents Television Council = Not Good Parents," Technology Liberation Front, November 22, 2004. www.techliberation.com.

For Further Discussion

Chapter 1

1. The Family Research Council, for which Suzanne Chamberlin works, promotes Christian values and formulates public policy that protects traditional marriage and the family. The American Civil Liberties Union works to defend citizens' rights, including freedom of expression. How might the missions of these two organizations affect their arguments regarding the effects of televised violence? Explain.

2. While Aubree Rankin contends that television can degrade viewers' values, Greg Asimakoupoulos claims that television can be used to teach people how to live more moral lives. Do you think TV shows that feature characters making ethical decisions can positively influence people? Can TV programs that glamorize immoral behavior negatively affect viewers' values? Explain.

3. Gregory Fouts and Kimberley Burggraf use numerous studies to bolster their assertion that females are degraded and stereotyped in television shows. Michael Abernathy supports his argument that television programs typecast males by offering examples that he has personally seen on television. Which type of evidence do you find more convincing, and why?

4. In Erik Meers's view, gays and lesbians on reality TV shows are breaking through common stereotypes. Dana Stevens, on the other hand, believes that reality shows only further typecast gays. Do reality TV programs harm or help gays' image, in your opinion? Support your answer using facts from the viewpoints.

Chapter 2

1. Whereas Ann Vorisek White faults television for harming children's cognitive development, Daniel McGinn heralds TV as a powerful learning tool. Which author do you think makes the best argument regarding television and learning? Why?

2. How do you think Ron Kaufman's credentials as the designer of the Kill Your Television Web site might be influencing his argument that TV viewing contributes to the obesity epidemic?

3. Cynthia M. Frisby maintains that some viewers tune in to reality TV because seeing real people achieve their goals and dreams is inspiring. Melanie Phillips, on the other hand, contends that watching reality shows dehumanizes viewers. With

which argument do you agree? Expand on your answer, using facts from the viewpoints.

4. All of the authors in this chapter presume that television has an impact on society, although they disagree on whether this effect is positive or negative. Do you concur with their assumption that television influences viewers? Why or why not? Defend your answer, citing from the viewpoints.

Chapter 3

1. The National Council on Alcoholism and Drug Dependence maintains that alcohol commercials are responsible for distorting children's perceptions of alcohol and persuading people to increase their alcohol consumption. On the other hand, Adam Thierer contends that alcohol ads do not increase consumption but merely encourage drinkers to prefer one brand of alcohol over another. In your opinion, which author makes the most convincing claim regarding the effects of alcohol advertising? Explain.

2. Both Peter Bart and the Pharmaceutical Research and Manufacturers of America (PhRMA) discuss the effects of the Food and Drug Administration's relaxation of advertising regulations in 1997. Was the resulting effect on television commercials for pharmaceuticals positive or negative, in your opinion? How so? Do you find the ads' lists of side effects offensive, as Bart does, or informative, as the PhRMA views them? Explain.

3. After reading the viewpoints in this chapter, do you feel that television advertising influences viewers? To what extent? Defend your answer, using information from the viewpoints.

Chapter 4

1. Joe Saltzman is an associate mass media editor and journalism professor, whereas Eva Arlia is an intern for Concerned Women for America, an organization dedicated to bringing biblical principles into public policy. Describe how each author's credentials are likely to shape his or her opinion on televised indecency.

2. Chris Cramer and Gwen Lister are both members of the press —Lister founded a newspaper, and Cramer heads CNN International News. Despite their similar professional backgrounds, Cramer encourages the occasional censorship of televised war coverage whereas Lister denounces it. Whose argument do you find more persuasive, and why?

3. While some authors in this chapter believe that government must regulate TV programming and TV broadcasters, others contend that the government should refrain from doing so. Do you feel that the government should step in when a media monopoly begins to affect the diversity of news and opinions presented to viewers? Should it punish broadcasters for airing indecent content? Defend your answers using facts from the viewpoints.

Organizations to Contact

The editor has compiled the following list of organizations concerned with the issues debated in this book. The descriptions are derived from materials provided by the organizations. All have publications or information available for interested readers. The list was compiled on the date of publication of the present volume; the information provided here may change. Be aware that many organizations take several weeks or longer to respond to inquiries, so allow as much time as possible.

Academy of Television Arts & Sciences
5220 Lankershim Blvd., North Hollywood, CA 91601
(818) 754-2800
Web site: www.emmys.org
Based in North Hollywood, the academy represents a range of television professionals from network executives to hair stylists who vote on nominees and winners for the annual Emmy Awards and College TV Awards. It publishes *Emmy Magazine* and sponsors events, workshops, and screenings of movies and miniseries. Its Archive of American Television, which produces a journal called the *Vault*, contains over four hundred interviews with actors, news anchors, producers, and other figures in the television industry.

Ad Council
261 Madison Ave., 11th Fl., New York, NY 10016
(212) 922-1500 • fax: (212) 922-1676
e-mail: info@adcouncil.org • Web site: www.adcouncil.org
The Ad Council is a nonprofit organization that works with businesses, advertisers, the media, and other nonprofit groups to produce and distribute public service advertisements, many of which are televised. The council also conducts research in order to improve the effectiveness of its campaigns. Studies and descriptions of its campaigns, which range from V-chip awareness to obesity prevention, can be found on its Web site.

Cato Institute
1000 Massachusetts Ave. NW, Washington, DC 20001
(202) 842-0200 • fax: (202) 842-3490
e-mail: cato@cato.org • Web site: www.cato.org
The institute is a libertarian public policy research foundation dedicated to promoting limited government, individual liberty, and free-market economics. It publishes the bimonthly *Policy Report* and the periodic *Cato Journal*. Cato's Web site provides access to policy

reports, legal briefs, the current issue and archives of its quarterly *Regulation*, and articles by Cato analysts, including "Rating Entertainment Ratings: How Well Are They Working for Parents, and What Can Be Done to Improve Them?"

The Caucus for Television Producers, Writers & Directors
PO Box 11236, Burbank, CA 11236
(818) 843-7572 • fax: (818) 846-2159
e-mail: BonnyInc@aol.com • Web site: www.caucus.org
The caucus represents producers, writers, and directors of cable and network television who believe that the American public is deserving of excellence in television programming. The Caucus Television Bill of Rights is posted on its Web site, in addition to news, opinions, a calendar of events, and a members-only bulletin board. The organization produces the *Journal of the Caucus*.

Center for Successful Parenting
PO Box 179, 1508 E. Eighty-sixth St., Indianapolis, IN 46240
e-mail: csp@onrampamerica.net • Web site: www.sosparents.org
Founded in 1998, the center was created to increase awareness of the negative effects of violence in the media on children and to encourage the public to help shield children from media violence. On its Web site, the center offers facts on televised violence, reports on the content of old and new movies, and numerous articles, including "Can Violent Media Affect Reasoning and Logical Thinking?"

Center on Alcohol Marketing and Youth (CAMY)
2233 Wisconsin Ave. NW, Suite 525, Washington, DC 20007
(202) 687-1019
e-mail: info@camy.org • Web site: www.camy.org
Based at Georgetown University, the Center on Alcohol Marketing and Youth focuses on the marketing practices of the alcohol industry, particularly those that may cause harm to America's youth. Its Web site features numerous studies and fact sheets on alcohol advertising as well as a gallery of liquor and beer commercials that it finds to be of concern. *Television: Alcohol's Vast Adland* is among its many reports.

Children's Advertising Review Unit (CARU)
70 W. Thirty-sixth St., 13th Fl., New York, NY 10018
(866) 334-6272, ext.111
e-mail: caru@caru.bbb.org • Web site: www.caru.org
As the children's branch of the U.S. advertising industry's self-regulation program, CARU examines ads aimed at children. It pro-

motes responsible children's advertising and corrects misleading or inaccurate commercials with the help of advertisers. The Web site provides access to commentary, articles, and news. One of its news releases that discusses TV commercials is "Burger King Shows Its Commitment to Kids."

Concerned Women for America (CWA)
1015 Fifteenth St. NW, Suite 1100, Washington, DC 20005
(202) 488-7000 • fax: (202) 488-0806
Web site: www.cwfa.org

Members of CWA work to strengthen the traditional family according to Judeo-Christian moral standards. The group supports the censorship of indecency and profanity on both broadcast and cable television. It publishes numerous brochures and policy papers as well as *Family Voice*, a monthly newsmagazine.

Federal Communications Commission (FCC)
1919 M St. NW, Washington, DC 20554
(888) CallFCC (225-5322) • (202) 418-0200
fax: (202) 418-0232
e-mail: fccinfo@fcc.gov • Web site: www.fcc.gov

The FCC is an independent government agency responsible for regulating telecommunications. It develops and implements policy concerning interstate and international communications by television, satellite, cable, radio, and wire. The FCC also reviews the educational programming efforts of the networks. Its various reports, updates, and reviews can be accessed on its Web site.

KidsHealth.org
The Nemours Foundation Center for Children's Health Media
1600 Rockland Rd., Wilmington, DE 19803
(302) 651-4046 • fax: (302) 651-4077
e-mail: info@kidshealth.org • Web site: www.kidshealth.org

The mission of KidsHealth.org is to help families make informed decisions about children's health by providing pediatric health information geared to children, teens, and parents. "How TV Affects Your Child" and "Restricting R-Rated Movies May Reduce Kids' Risk of Smoking" are two of the numerous publications available on its Web site.

MediaChannel.org
575 Eighth Ave., New York, NY 10018
(212) 246-0202 • fax: (212) 246-2677
e-mail: info@mediachannel.org
Web site: www.mediachannel.org

MediaChannel.org, a nonprofit Web site, explores global media issues. In addition to news, commentaries, reports, and discussion forums, the site provides articles on children's advertising, TV news journalism, and public television. One of its news alerts is titled "Public Loses Twice: FCC Promotes Indecency, Then Censors It."

Media Coalition
139 Fulton St., Suite 302, New York, NY 10038
(212) 587-4025 • fax: (212) 587-2436
e-mail: mediacoalition@mediacoalition.org
Web site: www.mediacoalition.org

The Media Coalition defends the American public's right to access the broadest possible range of opinion and entertainment, including violent or sexually explicit material that is considered offensive or harmful. It opposes a government-mandated ratings system for television. On its Web site, the coalition provides legislative updates and reports, including *Shooting the Messenger: Why Censorship Won't Stop Violence.*

MediaWatch
PO Box 618, Santa Cruz, CA 95061-0618
(800) 631-6355
e-mail: info@mediawatch.com • Web site: www.mediawatch.com

MediaWatch challenges racism, sexism, and violence in the media through education and action. It does not believe in censorship but helps create more informed consumers of the mass media and a more active citizenry by distributing media literacy information. It makes available books, newsletters, and educational videos, such as *Don't Be a TV: Television Victim.* On its Web site, MediaWatch provides current news and commentary on media issues, including the article "Murder, Sex, Mayhem: Tonight at Six."

Morality in Media (MIM)
475 Riverside Dr., Suite 239, New York, NY 10115
(212) 870-3222 • fax: (212) 870-2765
e-mail: mim@moralityinmedia.org
Web site: www.moralityinmedia.org

Established in 1962, MIM is a national, not-for-profit interfaith organization that works to combat obscenity and to uphold decency standards in the media. It maintains the National Obscenity Law Center, a clearinghouse of legal materials, and sponsors public information programs to involve concerned citizens. The *Morality in Media Newsletter* and the handbook *TV: The World's Greatest Mind-Bender* are published by MIM.

National Association of Broadcasters (NAB)

1771 N St. NW, Washington, DC 20036
(202) 429-5300 • fax: (202) 429-4199
e-mail: nab@nab.org • Web site: www.nab.org

NAB is a trade association representing the interests of radio and television broadcasters. It keeps its members abreast of technological developments, management trends, and research into matters related to the broadcasting of television, satellite, digital TV, and radio. Its Web site contains press releases, position statements, studies on audience viewing habits, legal testimonies, and information about public service campaigns. NAB's members receive weekly e-mail publications entitled *RadioWeek* and *TV Today* as well as the monthly newsletters *Associate Monthly* and *NAB World*.

National Cable & Telecommunications Association (NCTA)

1724 Massachusetts Ave. NW, Washington, DC 20036
(202) 775-3550
Web site: www.ncta.com

Founded in 1952, the NCTA is the principal trade association of the cable television industry in the United States. The NCTA's primary mission is to provide its members with a strong national presence and a unified voice on issues affecting the cable and telecommunications industry. Speeches, reports, and judicial filings can be accessed on its Web site. Members of the association also receive special reports and newsletters.

National Coalition Against Censorship (NCAC)

275 Seventh Ave., New York, NY 10001
(212) 807-6222 • fax: (212) 807-6245
e-mail: ncac@ncac.org • Web site: www.ncac.org

NCAC is an alliance of national nonprofit organizations, including literary, artistic, religious, educational, and civil liberties groups. The coalition is united by a conviction that freedom of thought, inquiry, and expression must be defended and that censorship of ideas must be opposed. NCAC's Web site provides press releases, legal briefs, congressional testimony on violence in the media, and background papers, such as "Censorship's Tools du Jour: V-Chips, TV Ratings, PICS, and Internet Filters."

Parents Television Council (PTC)

707 Wilshire Blvd., Los Angeles, CA 90017
(800) 882-6868 • fax: (213) 629-9254
e-mail: editor@parentstv.org • Web site: www.parentstv.org

The goal of PTC is to ensure that American television programming is values driven. PTC produces an annual *Family Guide to Prime Time Television* that profiles every sitcom and drama on the major television networks and provides information on subject matter that is inappropriate for children. On its Web site, the PTC posts movie reviews, television analysis: "Best and Worst of the Week," articles, and special reports. Its members receive the monthly newsletter, *PTC Insider.*

Society for the Eradication of Television (SET)
PO Box 10491, Oakland, CA 94610-0491
(510) 763-8712

Members of SET oppose television and encourage others to stop all television viewing. The society believes television "retards the inner life of human beings, destroys human interaction, and squanders time." SET maintains a speakers bureau and reference library and publishes manuals and pamphlets, the periodic *Propaganda War Comix*, and the quarterly *SET Free: The Newsletter Against Television.*

TV Turnoff Network (formerly TV-Free America)
1601 Connecticut Ave. NW, Suite 303, Washington, DC 20009
(202) 518-5556 • fax: (202) 518-5560
e-mail: e-mail@tvturnoff.org • Web site: www.tvturnoff.org

TV Turnoff Network is a national nonprofit organization that encourages Americans to reduce the amount of television they watch in order to promote stronger families and communities. It sponsors the annual National TV-Turnoff Week, when millions of Americans forego television for seven days, as well as a reading program called More Reading, Less TV. The organization prints a triannual newsletter, the *TV-Free American.*

Bibliography of Books

Robert C. Allen and Annette Hill, eds.	*The Television Studies Reader.* New York: Routledge, 2003.
Ben H. Bagdikian	*The New Media Monopoly.* Boston: Beacon, 2004.
Myrna Blyth	*Spin Sisters: How the Women of the Media Sell Unhappiness—and Liberalism—to the Women of America.* New York: St. Martin's, 2004.
Tim Brooks and Earle F. Marsh	*The Complete Directory to Prime Time Network and Cable TV Shows, 1946–Present.* New York: Ballantine, 2003.
Joanne Cantor	*"Mommy, I'm Scared": How TV and Movies Frighten Children and What We Can Do to Protect Them.* San Diego: Harvest/Harcourt Brace, 1998.
Joe Cappo	*The Future of Advertising: New Media, New Clients, New Consumers in the Post-Television Age.* New York: McGraw-Hill, 2003.
Louis Chunovic	*One Foot on the Floor: The Curious Evolution of Sex on Television from* I Love Lucy *to* South Park. New York: TV Books, 2000.
William Cote and Roger Simpson	*Covering Violence.* New York: Columbia University Press, 2000.
Gene Del Vecchio	*Creating Ever-Cool: A Marketer's Guide to a Kid's Heart.* Gretna, LA: Pelican, 1998.
Wheeler Winston Dixon, ed.	*Film and Television After 9/11.* Carbondale: Southern Illinois University Press, 2004.
Jon Dovey	*Freakshow: First Person Media and Factual Television.* London and Sterling, VA: Pluto, 2000.
Jib Fowles	*The Case for Television Violence.* Thousand Oaks, CA: Sage, 1999.
Jonathan L. Freedman	*Media Violence and Its Effect on Aggression: Assessing the Scientific Evidence.* Toronto: University of Toronto Press, 2002.
James Friedman	*Reality Squared: Televisual Discourse on the Real.* New Brunswick, NJ: Rutgers University Press, 2002.
Frank Furedi	*Paranoid Parenting: Why Ignoring the Experts May Be Best for Your Child.* Chicago: Chicago Review Press, 2001.
David Gauntlett	*Media, Gender, and Identity: An Introduction.* New York: Routledge, 2002.

Todd Gitlin

Media Unlimited: How the Torrent of Images and Sounds Overwhelms Our Lives. New York: Metropolitan Books, 2002.

Felix Gutierrez, Clint Wilson, and Lena Chao

Racism, Sexism, and the Media: The Rise of Class Communication in Multicultural America. Thousand Oaks, CA: Sage, 2003.

Justin Healey, ed.

Overweight and Obesity. Balmain, Australia: Spinney, 2004.

Su Holmes and Deborah Jermyn, eds.

Understanding Reality Television. New York: Routledge, 2004.

Richard M. Huff

Reality Television. Westport, CT: Praeger, 2005.

Gerard Jones

Killing Monsters: Why Children Need Fantasy, Super Heroes, and Make-Believe Violence. New York: Basic Books, 2002.

Kaiser Family Foundation

Shouting to Be Heard: Public Service Advertising in a New Media Age. Washington, DC: Kaiser Family Foundation, 2002.

Jeffrey P. Koplan, Catharyn T. Liverman, and Vivica I. Kraak, eds.

Preventing Childhood Obesity: Health in the Balance. Washington, DC: National Academies Press, 2005.

Robert Kubey

Creating Television: Conversations with the People Behind Fifty Years of American Television. Mahwah, NJ: Lawrence Erlbaum Associates, 2000.

Lawrence Lessig

Free Culture: How Big Media Uses Technology and the Law to Lock Down Culture and Control Creativity. New York: Penguin, 2004.

Hugh Mackay

Media Mania: Why Our Fear of the Modern Media Is Misplaced. Sydney, Australia: UNSW Press, 2002.

William J. Mann

Behind the Screen: How Gays and Lesbians Shaped Hollywood, 1910–1969. New York: Viking, 2001.

Greg McLaughlin

The War Correspondent. Sterling, VA: Pluto, 2002.

Susan Murray and Laurie Ouellette, eds.

Reality TV: Remaking Television Culture. New York: New York University Press, 2004.

Nieman Foundation

Nieman Reports: Coverage Before and During the War in Iraq. Cambridge, MA: Harvard University Press, 2003.

Laurie Ouellette

Viewers Like You? New York: Columbia University Press, 2002.

J. Pels and David Stewart, eds.

Marketing in a Global Economy. Chicago: American Marketing Association, 2000.

Michael Tracey   *The Decline and Fall of Public Service Broadcasting.* Oxford: Oxford University Press, 1998.

Marie Winn   *The Plug-in Drug: Television, Computers, and Family Life.* 25th Anniversary Edition. New York: Penguin, 2002.

Katherine Young and Paul Nathanson   *Spreading Misandry: The Teaching of Contempt for Men in Popular Culture.* Montreal: McGill-Queen's University Press, 2001.

Index

is protected by the Constitution, 30–31

possible benefits of, 28–30

on reality TV, 23–25

regulating, must endure strict scrutiny, 30

research on, is inconclusive, 27–28

viewers will copy behavior from, 20–21

viewing, exaggerated fears about dangers in the world from, 21

watched by "values voters," 17–18

youths' exposure to, 17, 20

harmful impact of, 73

Walker, Jesse, 184

Warren, Ron, 14

wartime footage

editing out gruesome parts of, 174–75

ethical and journalistic issues on, 173

live coverage and, 173–74

manipulation of, 177

misinformation and exaggeration in, 178–79

must be shown as it really is, 178

public opinion polls on, 174

public support for the war and, 177–78

showing unedited, 174, 175

Weakest Link, The (TV series), 20

Weir, Presley, 101

West, Diana, 18

White, Ann Vorisek, 71

Whited, Lana, 53

Wiggles, The (TV series), 83

Wilcox, Brian, 20

Will & Grace (TV series), 60

Winn, Marie, 84

women, "thin ideal" of, 41–42

see also female characters

Yale University Family Television and Consultation Center, 75

Young, Katherine, 50

youth

alcohol advertising to, 133

effect of, does not justify ban on liquor ads, 137–38

negative consequences of, 134

reality of, 138

campaign promoting physical activity to, 89–90

censoring TV programs from, 13–14

cognitive development of, 73–74

copy aggressive behavior seen on TV, 20–21

food wars by, 95–96

impact of "thin ideal" female stereotype on, 41–42, 46–47

indecent programming and, 170

junk food advertising for, 128

merchandise sold from programs for, 80

not watching TV, benefits of, 12–13

reality TV viewing by, lessons learned from, 34

before TV, 72

TV programs for

learning from, 83

length of, 83

quality preschool, 78–79

research for producing educational, 81–83

shortcomings in, 85

wholesome, 17

TV viewing by

amount of time spent for, 72

can be an intellectual activity, 79–80

debate on effects of, 84–85

harmful health effects of, 90–91

harmful impact of, 72–73, 74–75

healthy alternatives to, 75–76

during mealtimes, 72

obesity is not to be blamed for, 97–98

parental monitoring of, 12

parents' reasons for, 86

recommendations for amount of time spent on, 74

research on effects of, 84

snacking and, 97

suppresses the imagination, 75–76

too much time is spent on, 90

violent, 17, 20

congressional concern over, 27

desensitization to violence and, 21–23

research on impact of, 27–28

Zoom (TV series), 85